EAST MEETS WEST:

Cover art by **Carol Christa**

THE TRANSPERSONAL APPROACH

Edited by **Rosemarie Stewart**

*This publication made
possible with the assistance of the Kern Foundation*

The Theosophical Publishing House
Wheaton, Ill. U.S.A.
Madras, India/London, England

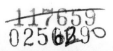

A Quest original. Published by the Theosophical Publishing
House, a department of the Theosophical Society in America.
Inquiries for permission to reproduce all or parts of this book
should be addressed to: Quest Books, 306 West Geneva
Road, Wheaton, Ill. 60187.

Library of Congress Cataloging in Publication Data

East meets West.
   "A Quest Original."
   Includes bibliographical references.
   1. Theosophy — Addresses, essays, lectures.
   2. Psychology — Addresses, essays, lectures. I. Stewart,
     Rosemarie, 1925 —
BP570.E2   299'.934   80-53952
ISBN 0-8356-0544-2   AACRI

Printed in the United States of America

CONTENTS

ACKNOWLEDGMENTS

We are grateful to *Main Currents in Modern Thought* for permission to reprint from their Vol. 23, No. 1, Sept./Oct. 1966 issue, the article by Dr. R. L. Sutherland, *East, West and Psychotherapy.*

Dr. Haridas Chaudhuri's contribution (Chapter 4), was previously published under a different title in the August 1978 edition of the *American Theosophist.*

The Source and the Seeker by Dr. Jean Raymond, was revised to her specifications. The article of the same name appeared first in the Special Spring 1979 issue of the *American Theosophist.*

Also from that 1979 Special Spring issue of the AT, was the article, *Defining Theosophical Psychology,* by Paul Herman, which he has revised and rewritten for this book.

The remaining chapters of this book were taken from the 1980 Special Spring issue of the AT and appear here in their original form with the exception of Chapter 5 by Martha Crampton who has revised her article.

We wish to acknowledge the fine work of Scott Miners, editor of the *American Theosophist,* in bringing these views and paradigms of such outstanding scholars and authors together.

— Rosemarie Stewart

Academic psychology is too exclusively Western. It needs to draw on Eastern sources as well. It turns too much to the objective, the public, the outer, the behavioral, and should learn more about the subjective, the private, the inner, the meditative. Introspection, thrown out as a technique, should be brought back into psychological research.

... By confining ourselves to the observation of external behavior, we overlook all sorts of human activities which do not show themselves externally in a simple form.

I should like to bring back introspection for another reason. We are discovering more and more, as we study personality in the depths rather than at the surface, that the deeper we penetrate the more universality we find. At men's deepest levels they seem to be more alike than different. Therefore, if the individual can touch these depths within himself, usually with the aid of a therapist, he discovers not only himself, but also the whole human spirit. The non-academic psychologists of the East have always known this; we in the West must learn it too.

— Abraham Maslow,
Main Currents in Modern Thought,
Vol. 13, No. 2, Nov. 1956, p. 27.

> 1 <

EAST, WEST AND PSYCHOTHERAPY
R. L. Sutherland, M.D.

For a long time, I have believed that a comparison of basic themes from West and East would have much to offer the practice of psychotherapy. I speak as a Westerner, with more to gain from the Orient than to offer. But in a conversation all sides stand to win.

What I shall refer to as "Oriental" is the way the Vendantist, Buddhist, and Taoist classically have viewed things, [1,2,3,4,5] as well as a few Westerners, like Hume, Emerson, and Whitehead. [6,7,8]

Of the many differences between the classical West and East, two are especially important for us here. First there is the contrast between dualism and non-dualism. The West has long held the view that reality is divided between the object and the subject, between the present and the remote, between time and space, between good and bad, and so on.

The non-dualism of the classical Orient, on the other hand, tends to view the world as a great organic *action* rather than a set of separate *things*, and sees the division between any one thing and all other things as a man-made construction for ease in communication and not inherently the nature of reality itself.

The second difference is the objective emphasis of the West versus the subjective viewpoint of the East. We in Europe and America take for granted that the real world "out there" is composed of what we can touch or see, things that hold still long enough for us to observe and record them; and we believe our observing mind is a mere reflector of this enduring reality of objects and situations.

The classical Oriental view, on the contrary, stresses the primacy of the experience or image. There is something like an *illusion* of the world; transitory impressions that only *seem* like an enduring something. The "mind" and the "person" also are mere constructs, eternally coming into being and perishing.

These two general differences in outlook have important implications for the nature of man and psychology. Modern Europe and America, at least prior to the very recent emphasis on existentialism, have derived their understanding of people from Western technical science. In the past century and a half, the most trusted sources of objective knowledge about man and his world have been physics, chemistry, biology, and, more recently, anthropology, sociology, and economics. In other words, we have believed in more or less stable, objective structures which can be described and organized. Then, as a consequence, we have taken for granted a meeting between subject and object. This is the purview of psychology. Assuming a world "out there," we want to know how a person encounters it, feels it, and decides about it.

Now, in contrast to this view, our classical Oriental sees a human *being* rather than a human *structure*. This being is expressed as a verb rather than as a noun, like "mind" or "soul." The human being is seen as creating the world by an act of choice. He is a "creating" rather than a creature. But here comes probably the hardest part of Oriental philosophy for a Westerner. Our dualism is so strong that we cannot conceive of an operation operating itself; we demand a doer as well as a doing.

Descartes, in his famous, "I think, therefore I am," tried to take nothing for granted except what was absolutely obvious. What is more obvious to one busily engaged in thinking than the fact that he thinks? But with our eyes opened by the Oriental sages and the existential philosophers, our twentieth century hindsight perceives that Descartes made a gratuitous assumption when he said "*I* think." There was a going on— of images, words, a flow of sights and sounds—remembered? anticipated?—we can't say; such events don't label themselves for us. And Descartes did what our tradition has done as far back as our written language goes: he took for granted that if there is an image there *must* be a mind, a person entertaining that image; if thinking, then *I* think.

Apparently, this was also the position in Asia about twenty-five hundred years ago. But the philosophers of Vedanta and Buddhism took hold of this assumption, "I think," and went a step further. "Thinking," they'd say, "but who am I who does it? And who am I who observes it?" Out of this question asked a million ways comes the non-dualism and the radical phenomenology of the Orient. Those two rather unfamiliar terms lead us to a very unfamiliar world.

As we have seen, non-dualism means figure and ground are all one piece, although we have chosen to see them as separate. We know this stair illusion and how, if we relax, it looks right-side-up for a few seconds, then upside-down, then back the first way. But we also know that if we *want* to see it a certain way, with a little effort we can shorten the time it stays in the other frame of reference. Thus we make the form of our reality. It isn't *in* the illusion-picture; we put it there. We invent it.

Similarly, with our question "Who thinks this thought?", there is no self-evident answer. To talk about it, our Western language invents a verbal subject. It says *"we"* look for a subject; and, of course, "we" see "ourselves" sitting here thinking about the problem. But—and some of us have done this in obsessive moments in our teens—the one who looks at us sitting here is a moment late; are we, indeed, thinking *this* thought? A dog trying to catch his tail, we see ourselves as we were a moment ago or imagine ourselves as we *might* be. We can't quite seize ourselves in the act of seizing ourselves. There is a figure in mind called "me" and a structure in this figure called "my mind." These are imaginary. We are a step beyond Descartes. All there ever is or can be is the *image,* never the subject, as he views the image.

3

When the separation of subject and object is seen purely as an invention, this is non-dualism. And when the only remaining datum is the image, the experience, the sensation, then this is radical phenomenology. (9,10) The image-experience, the moment of consciousness, is the only thing from which comes a sense of continuity, a conviction of self-identity, and a structured world.

From the philosophical difference between the two sides of the earth come two ways to treat human problems.

The Western approach is in terms of structure. We change circumstances: this is the province of sociology, engineering, medicine, and the like. Or we change the person; and for psychotherapy this means the "mind." We try to make "it" more flexible, free of habitual impairments, broader and deeper.

But whether the change is in environment or mind, we Westerners see organizations or machines to be modified. These may be institutions like the state, the economic system, the school, the corporation, or the family. They may be certain people in the environment who are to be induced to act differently. They may be bodily structures, such as muscles, the brain, or the circulatory system. And, for the psychotherapist, they are mental structures—the conscious, the unconscious, the instincts, memory systems, conditioned reflexes, and the like. These are to be strengthened, re-shaped, or made to act better. In short, some *thing* is to be analyzed, then corrected.

In contrast to this attack on structures, the classical Vedantist, Buddhist, or Taoist emphasis is on ways of experiencing. Here synthesis takes the place of analysis. The private world of each person is to be seen in a different light. This comes about by clearing away obstacles to a fuller awareness. It requires concentration and meditation. The goal of the various practices of the Vedantists and Buddhists is always to open up what is potentially "there," like the eyes penetrating a fog bank, in contrast to our more familiar process of building and repairing. The being or self is not so much to be repaired like a faulty structure taken down part by part and rearranged or added-on to, as it is to *emerge* as an ever-changing experience, by means of sharpened consciousness. And we must remember that even this self is a set of image-experiences, transitory, always coming into being anew.

The implication is that back of *my* being there is Being itself, that in discovering how transitory is the momentary *me*, a glimpse will come of the enduring, nameless Self which belongs to no one and which we all are. In this is found peace, happiness, and freedom. But we can't get it by proving it or identifying it—only by opening up to it.

Obviously, understanding the contrast between these world-views is important, for each is basic to the values and actions of a vast population.

If the Western therapist were to move in the direction of the Easterner, he would emphasize more the here-and-now experience of his patient. He would, for instance, see memory not so much a mirroring of "facts" in the past as something being made on the spot, a set of images belonging to this moment just as much as if they referred to a painful finger, a work of fiction, or the expectation of day-after-tomorrow. He would ask his patient to pay attention to the creative choices available to him, particularly in his attitudes toward memory, expectation, and present observation. These choices are much wider to one who sees a potential world of images, feelings, and attitudes being created this moment than to one who emphasizes the objective "out there" reality as if it were only one way and pretty well locked up by circumstances. "What do you want to do about it?" is a more Oriental question than, "How did you get this way?" and "How do you choose to feel?" is more Asian in tone than, "How do you feel?"

We tend to think of the Eastern holy man as a woolly-headed fellow far from the world of what really matters. For him, human happiness is what counts. To what avail are good plumbing, cures for trachoma, and democratic government unless they lead to happiness? He thinks constant attention to the mental state is the direct line to happiness and that *without* it all the changes we can make in economics, surgery, and enlightened family relations will do no good at all. He often thinks that *with* it our Western manipulations are gilding the lily.

He may be too direct in his approach; but there is something very practical about going to the heart of a problem.

Western tradition has largely turned from the philosophers who stress awareness, understanding, and patient acceptance of nature, to the technologists, who tell us how to master nature and change it. We in the Occident are practical in our handling of *things*, but rather impractical in our so-called pursuit of happiness.

The Western therapist has something to gain from the literature and example of the Vedantists, the Buddhists, and the Taoists: something of their basic quiet, their radical acceptance of the tragic moment as well as the lucky one, their faith in an order beyond technology and world politics, beyond anything the mind can grasp — something of their techniques in meditation, of seriously asking questions they know can't be answered but that lead to new ways of knowing. These are nearer the psychotherapist's practices of free association, non-judgmental listening, and emphasis on the therapeutic moment, than to other departments of Western life. (II) We are somewhat closer to the Orient than is the engineer or the surgeon and can come closer still.

Certainly the Easterner will continue his recent swing toward the Occident in improving the streets, the food supply, and the schools. He is absorbing our ways faster than we are using his. But when either of us tries really to understand the other culture we run into obstructions.

In the West, the effort to analyze a problem into its parts leads to suspicion of anything like syncretism, "oceanic feeling," or mysticism. The model of a science based on impersonal, repeatable operations causes distrust of personal, unique experiences, which cannot be repeated, which are hard to define, and which are taken on faith.

I do not know how the Asian really feels about our Western ways. Besides, we are talking about a certain classical Eastern view — a now almost theoretical model we suspect lies in the depth of an Oriental mind often Westernized on the surface. We imagine that a person who sees time and spirit in endless, super-personal terms will find relatively little value in individual actions. From his point of view, the human being is identical with the universe and his choices make so little difference in it that Tom, Dick, or Harry may be only an intrusion on the cosmic scene. He may recoil from the Western view of the world as a kind of machine from which, at least in modern times, the ruling divinity has disappeared.

In brief, the West is concerned with the individual more in time than in eternity and may lose sight of the transpersonal and the eternal, while the classic East has been more concerned with a vast and fateful movement and may lose interest in our suffering patient.

We would like to develop a psychotherapy which sees the acutely troubled John or Mary as important but also values the eternal in him and allows in each moment some profound meaning which goes beyond the individual. The Western psychotherapist can use some of his Eastern brother's patient meditation, his emphasis on the unique and subjective, and his awareness of divinity and deep personal meaning in the universe beyond the individual. The Eastern teacher-philosopher can borrow from the Westerner something of his stress on the time-centered sense of individual worth, and his effort to improve society and bodily conditions, however transitory these changes may be.

I have elsewhere (13,14) urged my colleagues to allow some room for another view than that of the nineteenth century physics and biology which have shaped our way of thinking about human nature. Modern physics has pointed another way but has become inaccessible to the mathematically unsophisticated. Some biologists have begun to describe something like what used to be called spirit; but our psychology is still far from finding a conceptual place for such ancient notions as soul and God, even with new names. These ideas remain important to many people. Some of us suspect they reflect old truths rather than old superstitions. But perhaps in order to explore this dimension we will have to use techniques of the East, such as meditation and patient waiting, rather than Western analysis and logical reasoning.

We have only begun to understand the positive side of the psyche. Creativeness, love, and the search for meaning may need something from the classical East for full understanding. I believe we can study these Oriental traditions and find them effective in our own growth and in helping our patients.

Bibliography

1 Conze, Edward, *Buddhism, Its Essence and Development,* Philosophical Library, New York, 1951
2. Waley, Arthur, *The Way and Its Power; A Study of the Tao Te Ching,* Grove Press, New York
3. Watts, Alan W., *The Way of Zen,* Pantheon, New York, 1957
4. Yutang, Lin, *The Wisdom of China and India,* Modern Library, New York, 1942
5. Zimmer, Heinrich, *Philosophies of India,* Bollengen Foundation, New York, 1951
6. Hume, David, *A Treatise of Human Nature,* 1739
7. Emerson, Ralph Waldo, *Essays,* 1841
8. Whitehead, Alfred North, *Symbolism, Its Meaning and Effect,* Macmillan, New York, 1927
9. Ellenberger, Henri F., A Clinical Introduction to Psychiatric Phenomenology and Existential Analysis in *Existence,* Ed. Rollo May et al., Basic Books, New York, 1958
10. Farber, Marvin, *Philosophical Essays in Memory of Edmund Husserl,* Harvard University Press, Cambridge, 1940
11. Perry, Ralph Barton, *The Thought and Character of William James,* Geo. Braziller, New York, 1954
12. Fromm, Erich, et al., *Zen Buddhism and Psychoanalysis,* Harper & Bros., New York, 1960
13. Sutherland, Richard L., Therapeutic Goals and Ideals of Health, *Journal of Religion and Health,* 3:119-135, 1964
14. Sutherland, Richard L., Choosing — As Therapeutic Aim, Method and Philosophy, *Journal of Existential Psychiatry,* 2:371-392, 1962

Dr. Sutherland, who was formerly a member of the faculty of the Menninger Foundation School of Psychiatry, has been a practicing psychiatrist in Oakland, California, since 1951. In addition to his own practice, he was acting psychiatrist for the Student Health Service of the University of California, and Diocesan psychiatrist for the Episcopal Diocese of California, when this paper was presented to the Seventh Western Divisional Meeting of the American Psychiatric Association, on Kauai, Hawaii, September 2, 1965. The general subject of the meeting was Intercultural Issues.

This article appeared in *Main Currents in Modern Thought,* Vol. 23, No. 1., Sept./Oct. 1966.

2

DEFINING THEOSOPHICAL PSYCHOLOGY
Paul E. Herman

In *Unfinished Animal,*[1] his study of the "Aquarian frontier,"
Theodore Roszak traces the roots of the emergent consciousness which has been of widespread interest and concern during the past decade. He credits Helena P. Blavatsky and Annie
Besant with significant early contributions to this "higher sanity." However, Roszak is perhaps the only significant scholar
who has begun to demonstrate the considerable influence of
these early theosophists as contributors to the new psycho-
spiritual therapies which are gaining recognition and prestige
so rapidly. While some perceptive historians have maintained
that modern depth psychology descends directly from the
work of the eighteenth century physician Anton Mesmer, few
have studied the theosophical movement and antecedent,

---

[1] Theodore Roszak, *Unfinished Animal: the Aquarian Frontier and the Evolution of Consciousness* (New York: Harper Colophon Books, c1975), pp.
115-125.

derivative, and parallel forms of occultism as a continuation of what Ellwood calls the "alternative reality tradition."[2]

Moreover, recognition of the full tradition behind the new East-West, psychospiritual therapies has been seriously impeded by the insistence of a majority of leading psychotherapists, including Carl Jung, that it would undermine the legitimacy of psychotherapy to admit its common roots with mysticism and metaphysics. In their opinion psychotherapy must identify exclusively with the narrow values of scientific empiricism, or "scientism" and the "natural science ideology."

A theosophically based psychology, as I conceive it, must challenge such a widespread, pervasive taboo and acknowledge its metaphysical lineage. A research team at the California Institute of Asian Studies, in San Francisco, is currently researching the interface between theosophy and depth psychology and developing the model of a contemporary psychology and therapy frankly rooted in the perennial metaphysics, which for the last century has taken the name of theosophy.[3] The following brief statement of some essential principles of theosophical psychology is a first attempt to explore them with an eye on their potential for application in the practice of therapy.

Theosophical psychology is a holistic view of human individuality; it includes not only the elements of body, instincts, emotions, mind, society, and culture generally considered in the various contemporary psychologies, but also elements which usually have been overlooked in modern times: the "higher," creative mental, intuitive, and spiritual dimensions within each human being. Theosophical psychology is founded upon a perennial metaphysics, expressed in different ways in different cultures and epochs, which concerns itself with the origin and end of all things, of the One Life and its many evolving derivative forms. To comprehend this metaphysics fully the student must use his intuitive con-

---

2 Robert Ellwood, Jr., *Religious and Spiritual Groups in Modern America* (Englewood Cliffs, N.J.: Prentice-Hall, c1973), pp. 42-87.

3 The name theosophy is itself rooted in the ancient spirituality of the Near East, the region of most intimate East-West encounter throughout history.

sciousness to extend awareness beyond the range of the concrete mind. While this metaphysics distinguishes between various levels of reality, states of being, and consciousness in order to place each element in its proper perspective within the total scheme, it nevertheless affirms that the fundamental Reality is a unitary whole. Thus it reconciles unity and diversity into a holistic vision of the world and human nature.

In all cultures and historical periods mystical experience and the metaphysical wisdom based upon it have declared that there is an ultimate unity and purpose in life; that there is one infinite Self; that each individual self is essentially at one with this infinite Self; and that human evolution is destined to reveal the Self as the "Supreme Identity" within each individual. Thus the person is a microcosm of the universal Whole; or, as the Judeo-Christian tradition maintains, God made all human beings in His image and likeness. According to this understanding of correspondence every particle of matter is an epitome of the Whole, and every finite reality is a symbol and expression of the essential Reality within and above it. Both beyond and within everything is one omnipresent Reality, devoid of attributes because every attribute imposes a limitation. Indeed, from the standpoint of the human being ultimate Reality can be conceived of only as "Void" or "Non-Being," because human beings can know things only through their limitations, whereas omnipresent Reality transcends all bounds and conditions even while It provides the ground for, and substance of, each temporary manifestation.

Thus the universe is the expression of a unitary Life, an infinite Self. This Self, which expresses Itself in and as the universe, projects into that universe innumerable epitomes of Itself, individual immortal essences, unitive selves, sparks of the universal Fire. Each "spark" is a spiritual essence, or monad, which through a process of involution followed by evolution becomes the innermost essence of each evolving being. The monad expresses its being over vast periods of time through a number of vehicles or conditioned states of consciousness.

No matter how many aspects, principles, or states of consciousness may be within the full human being, that being is always a unity of awareness, just as the cosmos, which

11

emanated from the transcendental Ground, is a unitary Whole. The unitive self of each individual reflects in its smaller scale the cosmic unity, as well as such other features of the cosmos as its rhythmic process, its multidimensionality, and its evolutionary unfoldment of latent potentialities.

The individual's spiritual essence, an ultimate unit of consciousness, represents a first step out of the universal into the realm of the unique, a first step out of homogeneous universality into the world of differentiation. Each essential being is at first unconscious of itself, but it gradually learns to know itself as a separate unit by experiencing relationships with external elements as it identifies with substantial forms.

Theosophical psychology views the universe as a bipolar continuum, or a spectrum stretched between two poles of unity and diversity, spirit and matter, universe and individual. By means of its complementarity the bipolar process generates cosmic energy. Many intermediate states, or "planes," come into being between the poles of extreme diversity and separation, which comprise the physical world, and the ultimate unity of the infinite Self. Such "planes" are both states of consciousness and functional complexes of form ranging from the most rarified "matter-energy" to the most dense. The planes beyond the physical are formed of a force and structure impalpable and imperceptible to the ordinary physical senses developed so far in human evolution; until the present only a relatively few mystics, visionaries, and clairvoyants have experienced them firsthand. It is likely that even the glimpses of many of these pioneers have been partial and sometimes inaccurate. As evolution proceeds into the future, consciousness of the more rarified planes or dimensions will become both more accurate and widespread; such an expansion of awareness will allow increasing freedom from the limitations of time, space, and separation, as now experienced. At present it is difficult to imagine a consciousness released from such limitations, but theosophy states that such development will come to all beings in due course, as it has already come to the highly evolved Beings who offer their spiritual guidance when individuals can truly profit from it.

The series of planes constitutes a great chain of being and consciousness which connects the infinite Self of the cosmos with each individual self. The densest of these states of consciousness lying within and immediately beyond the physical realm have been studied scientifically by a few modern parapsychologists, paraphysicists, and depth psychologists; yet even so this field of investigation is barely launched.

The evolving beings who inhabit the present universe gradually achieve consciousness, and then self-consciousness, at every level and state of consciousness within the universe. All are destined at some time in their age-long evolution to master the complete scale of existence which lies between the individual and the universal. All will become fully conscious of their complete identity with the infinite Self, the Self which is the Supreme Identity of each individual.

Such expansion of consciousness and self-awareness takes place through a process in which the units of consciousness become identified with successive forms of increasing complexity and manifest intelligence. As the evolving beings increase their power of response they express themselves through more and more highly organized forms, first mineral forms, then vegetable forms, and on through animal and human forms, to suprahuman forms. The forms themselves are mutable and mortal; so they are outlived and die when they have provided the appropriate experiences; yet the incarnating being persists beyond them. The indwelling consciousness continues to expand through the outer pattern of evolving forms. Even in the case of radical discontinuities, mutations, missing links, extinction of species, destruction of whole continents such as biological and cultural evolutionists have studied, nothing essential is lost as the unfolding identity develops its whole nature through the use of forms. While the evolving being retains every capacity and power of response it has developed while inhabiting the successive embodiments, it renews itself through a ceaseless process of birth, death, and rebirth. Thus all the apparent reverses and advances, failures and successes in the dialectic of life are purposeful and valuable.

The individual essences pass through various forms as the mineral, vegetable, and animal phases of experience give way to human individualization. On entering the human state the evolving selves discover their innate divinity; at first very faintly, they become aware that while their animal nature is still strong and undeniable, they are indeed "gods in the becoming."

The human being is an individualized self, not merely conscious but also self-conscious. Even at a very primitive state of development he has within himself the ability to remember and compare, analyze and synthesize. So he develops powers of conceptual thought and becomes capable of choice and free will. He becomes proactive as well as reactive. He becomes capable of making mistakes, because only the human being can experiment, test by trial and error, and choose with great mental awareness.

The process of developing unified selfhood constitutes a great arc, a path of unconscious outgoing followed by the drama of conscious life. Through the increased self-awareness which results from this experience the human being eventually embarks upon a self-conscious return to the Source. The involutionary-evolutionary arc has been described as a path which leads from unconscious perfection, through conscious imperfection, to conscious perfection. First comes the phase of the unconscious, automatic perfection of rainbows and clouds, trees and flowers, deer and rabbits, and young children. Then comes the phase of conscious human imperfection, of freedom to learn through trial and error, of developing individual will-to-growth through choice; this phase is represented by the period of adolescence in the human cycle. Finally comes the phase of conscious perfection, of the maturity and integration of all parts of the being which have been mastered through self-knowledge. This last phase of full human potential is not actually achieved by many persons in the present stage of social and psychological evolution.

According to theosophical psychology the human being is a somewhat complex spectrum of consciousness and form which reflects exactly, in total expression, the evolving multidimensionality of the cosmos. Even though the person most often believes that his self-identity is more or less confined to the psychophysical organism, he is actually in process of becoming conscious on many levels, or states. The instinctual, emotional, and mental are only a beginning. As he gains expanded awareness he becomes conscious that his ultimate nature as an individual is the unitive Self, the spark of the divine Fire, the consciousness in which he experiences perfect identity with the infinite Self. In this unitive Self he realizes that the God within and the God without are one; thus even events and circumstances which seem to come unbidden from outside are really deliberate choices of the evolving self-nature. Subjective and objective, self and not-self, and all other bipolar pairs, are destined to achieve reintegration in the unitive Self.

The unitive Self can be pictured as standing on the threshold of the universal and gazing out into the world of multiplicity; sometimes it is said to possess the "I AM" consciousness. Yet the unitive Self projects into the world of diversity an expression of itself which distinctly belongs to that world. In the human state this essence is the transpersonal self, which is sometimes called the "I AM I" consciousness because it belongs to a level of awareness where boundaries and individuality, although perceived organically and holistically, are actual. The transpersonal self has three aspects, which can be spoken of as spiritual will-energy, superconscious wisdom-love, and active intelligent creativity. The "will" aspect is the individual awareness of the truth of the unitive Self, of the "Father in Heaven." Yet this spiritual will-energy also provides guidance for the next steps in one's transformation, and it carries along with it the intuition which unfolds awareness of ultimate destiny. The experiences of the person who is awakened to his spiritual nature give many clues which prove that everything which occurs in his life is in some sense chosen by his evolving transpersonal self.

The "wisdom" aspect of the transpersonal self has been referred to as the "Christ within," the universal principle of love which must be born within every human being and become for him "the way, the truth, and the life" in his task of reconciling the unique with the universal and unitive. It can be called the person's superconscious field. The third aspect, "activity," can be called creative mind; in conjunction with spiritual will-energy and superconscious wisdom-love it creates a recurrent partial expression of the transpersonal self. This creation is the personality, which again is triune. The personality consists of three major parts: mind, emotion and instinct, and physique. At the level of the personality the consciousness is that of "I am So-and-So."

15

Over and over the real individual, the immortal transpersonal self, as it evolves toward more expansive and holistic consciousness, puts forth a personality into the material world and thereby gradually learns the laws of life, cosmic Whole, and unitive Self through successive physical incarnations. After each incarnation the transpersonal self withdraws and dissolves the personality as it assimilates its experiences and transmutes them into higher values and capacities. Then, after a rest in the inward bliss of temporary and relative completeness, it turns outward once more to express itself through another personality under the great universal law of cycles, of outbreathing and inbreathing, of systole and diastole.

The personality remembers previous incarnations only through the immortal transpersonal self, and since most personalities in this world are far from full expressions of the transpersonal self, such memories are rare and spasmodic. The needs of evolving begins in an age-long experiment to master the universe through free will and choice of spiritual essence, are met through continuing vast cycles of changing races, religions, civilizations, cultures, and environments on this and other planets. All of this exuberant activity represents a kind of cosmic art work in progress.

Theosophical psychology can support a therapy which is based upon the spiritual practices of modern theosophy, often called the "path of discipleship." The process involves living a life of creative altruism, practicing brotherhood in daily relationships, and through choice shifting the center of self-identity from the personality to the transpersonal self. Such a shift replaces the exclusive impression that "I am So-and-So" with the conviction that "I am I," an eternally expanding transpersonal self who is at one with the essence of the cosmos and rooted in the transcendent Ground of existence. Psychological crises are often the call of the transpersonal self for such a radical shift from self-centeredness in the outer realm of consciousness to a conviction of self-identity and the spiritual unity of all human beings. Theosophical therapy includes a healing experience whose essential nature is just such a shift.

How can theosophical psychology be translated into the operational terms of practical therapy? While the process of a uniquely theosophical therapy cannot yet be charted with certainty, some important aspects of it can be discussed in preliminary fashion. The following elements appear to be central in it: 1) the transpersonal helping relationship; 2) creative altruism; 3) fair-witnessing; 4) assessment; 5) uncovering the conditioning process; 6) disidentification from personal self and experiential discovery of the transpersonal identity; 7) charting the myth of meaning for this incarnation; and 8) use of such imaginative techniques as that of "the white light." These factors will be described briefly in the following paragraphs.

1) TRANSPERSONAL HELPING RELATIONSHIP. The helping relationship is of great importance in such professions as medicine (including psychiatry), professional psychology, social work, counseling, and nursing. The science of the helping relationship stresses optimal ways of establishing a highly functional interaction between helper and helpee. The quality of the personal interaction is highly significant in any therapeutic relationship. But relationships are not only personal; they can also be transpersonal, or centered at the very deep level of identity on which the possibility of spiritual transmutation is much more likely. If the theosophical therapist's process of transpersonalizing his own consciousness has advanced significantly, he can clarify and greatly facilitate the possibility of his clients undergoing a parallel transformation.

2) CREATIVE ALTRUISM. The transpersonal helping relationship is a special example of something much broader in scope: living a life which emphasizes self-giving for the common welfare, which places the welfare of others ahead of the self-seeking tendency so natural at a certain level of human evolution, but which becomes dysfunctional in situations where social harmony is of importance, as it is in today's world. The theosophical therapist must strive to offer his skills and spiritual support without allowing the attitude of "me and mine first" to intrude. Consequently the therapist must work on himself to unmask all self-seeking attitudes and behaviors, however unconscious and ingeniously rationalized. Only as he becomes increasingly successful in this endeavor does he deserve the title of theosophical therapist. His consciousness, wisdom, and life style are unavoidably tested for quality when he sets himself up as a theosophical therapist.

3) FAIR-WITNESSING. The perspective of the "fair-witness" is stressed in Assagioli's psychosynthesis. This principle is very

close to one stressed in Krishnamurti's teachings and in the Vipassana meditation of Theravada Buddhism. The fair-witness, or "bystander mind," position is a relatively detached and nonjudgmental awareness of psychological and physical processes which opens the individual to fresh insights concerning himself and his characteristic ways of thought and interaction. The theosophical therapist who has made fair-witnessing a central part of his own experience is best able to model and teach this valuable therapeutic aid.

4) ASSESSMENT. Both initial and ongoing assessment of the client's personal and transpersonal situations is also highly important. Assessment is not the same as taking a diagnostic case history, which can stamp in more deeply the destructive conviction that one is determined by his personal life experiences. When properly employed, assessment objectifies the personality, noting both developed and latent powers, thereby freeing it for progressive change and transformation. Assessment should be combined with the process of fair-witnessing.

5) UNCOVERING THE CONDITIONING PROCESS. Through its interactions with significant persons, teachings, and identifications, each personality has been conditioned into certain habitual ways of perceiving and behaving. A person's entire conditioning can be objectified and then outgrown in its most destructive aspects. Nonevaluative watching is the method by which the full context of conditioning can come to consciousness. N. Sri Ram and Rohit Mehta are among the modern theosophical writers who have been significantly influenced by Krishnamurti's teaching, and they have described the conditioning and uncovering processes at length. The result of objectifying the conditioning process is a gradual dropping away of the more destructive aspects of the personality.

6) DISIDENTIFICATION AND EXPERIENTIAL DISCOVERY OF THE TRANSPERSONAL IDENTITY. As the body, desires, aversions, emotions, and mental conditioning process are more and more objectified, a shift of consciousness inward to the transpersonal focal point of identity becomes possible. Such an aspiration is illustrated in Geoffrey Hodson's meditation, the "yoga of light," which is one expression of a central theosophic psychospiritual practice. Shifting the center of consciousness inward to a free and energetic balance point is a possible ac-

complishment for many people, even though it may be difficult. The process can be successful if it involves the client's spiritual will, intuition, and fair-witnessing of his successes and regressions in the long-term transmutation process.

7) CHARTING THE MYTH OF MEANING FOR THIS INCARNATION. Each life has an inner meaning which can be understood only by the quiet, inwardly questing mind. Learning to listen to inner guidance is an extremely valuable method in theosophical therapy. Ways of facilitating the process of inner guidance through various kinds of meditative practice need to be explored by careful experimental evaluation.

8) USE OF IMAGINATIVE TECHNIQUES, INCLUDING THE WHITE LIGHT. Using symbolic visualization, while not entirely novel today, is very important in the practice of theosophical therapy. Transpersonal images are of great aid in demonstrating to clients the finer, more evolved parts of their being. Intuitive and creative abilities, as well as the inner guidance process, can be enhanced by the selective use of both directed and spontaneous imagery. "White light" techniques, such as those used in Agni Yoga, are worth exploring, even though they need to be used with caution.[4]

Paul E. Herman, Ph.D., is Professor of Internal Counseling Psychology, and the Director of the Integral Counseling Center, California Institute of Asian Studies in San Francisco.

He holds his graduate degrees from the University of California, Berkeley, Columbia University, Temple University, and the California Institute of Asian Studies. His Ph.D. is in Integral psychology. He is a California-licensed psychotherapist.

This article is revised from the original which was published in the *American Theosophist,* Spring issue, 1979.

---

[4] The fine, comprehensive survey of modern theosophical teachings which comprises pages seventy through one hundred and eighty-one of Hugh Shearman's *Modern Theosophy* (2nd ed.; Adyar, India: Theosophical Publishing House, 1954) has been most helpful in formulating the preceding statement. The outline of the middle portion of this essay follows Shearman's text closely in integrating metaphysical, cosmological, and psychological principles. However, I have revised terminology freely when I felt that earlier theosophical terms would be puzzling to the contemporary reader, whose familiarity is with depth psychology rather than late nineteenth and early twentieth century theosophical documents.

$$\Longrightarrow 3 \Longleftarrow$$

IN SEARCH OF SHUNYATA
Walt Anderson

One of the nice things about writing as a profession is that it introduces you to new things and also sometimes provides you with an impetus for going more deeply into subjects than you might have otherwise. That happened to me as I became involved in writing an introductory book about Tibetan Buddhism.[1] I had been interested in Buddhism for over ten years and had done a fair amount of study and practice in it, but, like most Westerners, had followed my interests and whims, and had not been required to come to grips with all aspects of it. One of the concepts I had touched on only lightly was *shunyata,* which seemed a most exotic notion, inscrutable and Oriental, that was not likely to be of much importance in my own life.

When I approached the job of writing a book about Buddhism — a project that evolved gradually out of some magazine articles I had written — I intended to concentrate on the subjects I knew best, particularly the parts of Buddhism that came closest to certain ideas in Western culture. As I got farther into it, I decided I should at least mention and define the basic concepts of Buddhism — and so, finally, I had to grapple with shunyata. In the process of doing so, I completely revised my ideas about its accessibility to the Western mind: Where I had once believed it to be a corner of Buddhism we might just as well leave unexplored, I now think it can be understood and that understanding it is the most direct path straight to the heart of Buddhism — and, more importantly, to a fundamental truth about nature and human consciousness.

Shunyata: The word translates usually as emptiness, sometimes voidness, the void, vacuousness, nothingness. It is used in two ways: to designate the great void, the source of all things which in Eastern cosmology is itself empty and without attributes; and to describe a state of mind in which emptiness or nothingness is *experienced*. These usages, especially the latter, tend to reinforce the idea held by many Westerners that Buddhists and yogis and so forth pursue a state of withdrawal from conscious experience, and generally espouse retreat from the real world in which people deal sensibly and practically with their problems.

The Buddhist scriptures that deal with the subject are difficult and sometimes, it would seem, deliberately contradictory. Consider the Prajna-paramite-hridaya Sutra, the "heart of great wisdom," which says, "emptiness does not differ from form, nor does form differ from emptiness; whatever is form, that is emptiness, whatever is emptiness, that is form."[2]

To say that form is emptiness and emptiness form appears, from a common-sense Western point of view, to be a profitless exercise in paradox. It is like saying up is down, black is white, in is out — yet this sutra is one of the most cherished writings in the Buddhist tradition, and surely it must be a serious attempt to communicate information.

But what information can there be in a statement that form is emptiness and emptiness form? When we think of form we associate it with objects, *things* that have shapes and sizes; for there to be form there must be *something* tangibly and visibly present; emptiness is the absence of *things*; it is open space, void.

The translation of shunyata that I found most helpful, that enabled me to glimpse a path through this apparent paradox, was Dr. Herbert Guenther's: no-thing-ness.[3] With the aid of a couple of hyphens, I could see a meaning that the word nothingness did not communicate: The state of mind described by the word shunyata is not so much one of black emptiness as one of thing-less but event-full flux and change; it is a consciousness of energy rather than matter, of verbs rather than nouns.

Buddhism is simultaneously a statement about the cosmos and a statement about the nature of the human mind. It is a system in which cosmology and psychology are not separated. Buddhism does not compartmentalize knowledge in the same way that we do, and this is one of the reasons we find it hard to understand.

I noticed, as I began studying Western interpretations of Buddhism, that at different times and places it had occupied different categories: Most people think of it as a religion — which is accurate enough, except that it has nothing whatever to say about God. Other people have chosen to view Buddhism as a non-theistic philosophy, concerned with such things as the inevitability of suffering in human life and the problem of attachment to material things. This approach, which has a certain stiff-upper-lip quality to it, has been especially popular in England. In the United States there has been a growing tendency to view Buddhism in psychological terms. Alan Watts, one of the most influential writers in this area, said that, if we look deeply into Eastern wisdom, "we do not find either philosophy or religion as these are understood in the West. We find something more nearly resembling a psychotherapy."[4] And recently we have discovered a fourth category: Such works as Fritjof Capra's *The Tao of Physics* have drawn our attention to the striking similarities between the ancient teachings of the East and the most recent theoretical formulations of modern physics.

Of course Buddhism is all these things — religion, philosophy, psychology, physics — and none of them; to ask which category it belongs in is to back oneself into a mental trap rather like the *koan* of Zen.

But although each categorization is partial and in a way distorting, each has at least enabled us to get another piece of the puzzle, and to make some progress in what I suspect will be regarded in the future as one of the great intellectual projects of human history: the synthesis of Eastern and Western thought.

The most recent development, the discovery of the connection between Eastern wisdom and modern physics, is one that I find especially interesting for two reasons: One, it gives us what is probably the best available Western concept equivalent to shunyata; and, two, it evidences some progress in the direction of a breakdown of the barrier between physics and psychology.

Physics — Old and New

The old physics, the physics of Isaac Newton, was a science of things: solid objects that occupied certain segments of space, "It seems probable to me," Newton wrote, "that God in the beginning formed matter in solid, massy, hard, impenetrable moving particles, of such sizes and figures, and with such other properties, and in such proportion to space, as most conduced to the end for which he formed them . . . ."[5] These basic building-blocks of the cosmos were, for Newton, durable and indestructable; and they occupied specific spaces for specific durations of time, regardless of what other bodies might be doing and regardless of the location of the observer. Underlying Newtonian physics was the Cartesian separation of subject from object, the *res cogitans* of mind from the *res extensa* of things.

Physics in this century has moved steadily away from Newton. As Capra puts it: "Two separate developments — that of relativity theory and of atomic physics — shattered all the principal concepts of the Newtonian world view: the notion of absolute space and time, the elementary solid particles, the strictly causal nature of physical phenomena, and the ideal of an objective description of nature."

The cosmos as described by modern physics is much more Buddhist than Newtonian: Matter turns out to be a condition of something — or nothing — that is also energy. Penetration into the depths of solid objects reveals vast spaces occupied by forces that appear and disappear, change shape, and are endlessly in motion. That which is form is emptiness; that which is emptiness, form. Shunyata — which seems so strange when we encounter it in the Buddhist scriptures — appears again in the "hardest" of the Western sciences. Consider, as an example of how far we have come from Newton, the following comment by Percy Bridgman, a nobel laureate in physics:

> It has always been a bewilderment to me to understand how anyone can experience such a commonplace event as an automobile going up the street and seriously maintain that there is identity of structure of this continually flowing, dissolving and reforming thing and the language that attempts to reproduce it with discrete units . . . .[7]

There are signs that, along with the Newtonian building-blocks, other parts of the classical scientific world-view are crumbling also: Werner Heisenberg has questioned the subject-object separation that is fundamental to our traditional notions of scientific fact-finding.[8] David Bohm raises the question that follows inevitably from that: Why separate physics from psychology? "The real material of theoretical physics," says Bohm, "is the nature of thought."[9]

Although these are remarkable developments, we should keep them in perspective; this more fluid, event-centered, rather than thing-centered view of physical reality, is not entirely new to Western culture. It is an ancient and persistent theme that has been expressed in many times and places. Remember Heraclitus: "In the same rivers we step and we do not step; we are and we are not."[10]

Such views are not alien to Western culture, and I doubt that a Newtonian or thing-centered world-view is alien to Eastern culture. The tendency to reify, to freeze events into things, to grasp at the flow of phenomena and try to rigidify it into something easier to control, is probably as common in the East as in the West; it is the source of the essential unsatisfactoriness, *dukkha,* which the Buddha described as the natural state of unenlightened human beings. And indeed the purpose of Buddhism is to enable people to break free of that tendency, to become liberated — to experience shunyata.

This is where the difference between East and West really lies: We are, in the West, so in awe of our machines that we believe they alone are capable of discovering the truth. It does not seem to have occurred to many physicists that the reality unfolded in their research and theory might be *experienced* by ordinary people; but Eastern mysticism has searched incessantly for ways that human beings might be enabled to let go of their thing-sickness and awaken to life in a universe of events. That, essentially, is what it is about: It is a body of knowledge — a technology, if you will — devoted to enabling people to learn to live in a fluid cosmos, insubstantial and transitory.

Techniques of Exploration

In the West we equate technology with machinery; the cosmos is explored with cyclotrons and lasers and telescopes. Eastern technology has been largely non-mechanical, relying on the apparatus of the disciplined human body and mind. The best-known of its exploratory methods is meditation: the act of being still and simply observing the breath or the flow of thoughts. This often upsets the beginning student: Nothing special happens, the attention wanders, thoughts come and go. The teachers and the scriptures insist that this is precisely what is to be observed, that it is the source of important knowledge. One text says:

> Since the One Mind is empty and without any foundation, the individual's mind is also as empty as the sky. To know whether this is so or not, look within your own mind . . . .
> Divine wisdom is indestructible and unbreakable, like the ever-flowing current of a river. To know whether this is so or not, look within your own mind.
> Since they are merely a flow of instability like the air, objective appearances are without power to fascinate and fetter. To know whether this is so or not, look within your own mind.[11]

The above passage from *The Tibetan Book of the Great Liberation* is typical of many writings on the subject of meditation. The message is essentially the same: The belief that things have substance and permanence is an illusion, a trick of your mind, and the illusion can be seen through; you look clearly, perceive the truth, and are set free. The truth is always there to be seen, never hiding, however much you may ignore it in your search for something — some *thing* — more resembling your idea of what a transcendent experience should be like.

Another exploratory method, closely akin to meditation, is the practice of systematic introspection. In traditional Buddhist teaching this was connected with the study of the *dharmas,* basic mental events. The dharma-system is a sophisticated approach to what we would today call phenomenology; it includes precise definitions of mental events such as sense-experiences, feeling-tones, states of attention and volition, and concentration and boredom. It is an exacting and highly cognitive discipline and one rarely explored by Western followers — an unfortunate omission, by the way, since it deprives us of a valuable part of the Buddhist heritage and tends to further the misconception that spiritual practice is an exclusively intuitive or "right brain" business in which the intellect plays no part. The dharmas are an atomic table of the psyche, representing what were taken to be the irreducible units of thought; they are used to focus on experience and precisely identify its components.[12] The goal of the practice is the same as that of meditation: one perceives the true nature of thought, and realizes that there is nothing in it which can be identified as a solid and permanent object — or a solid and permanent subject. Newtonian things and the personal ego both fall beneath the sword (as Buddhist texts frequently describe it) of discriminating awareness.

The dharma system was devised as a tool to be used against the reifying tendencies of the human mind, but those tendencies are so powerful that many scholars fell into the trap of regarding the dharmas themselves as things rather than as descriptions of events. This was why their use was discontinued by some Buddhist schools (i.e., Zen), and this is why the Prajna-paramite-hridaya Sutra includes the reminder that "all dharmas are marked by emptiness."

There are other techniques for cutting through the illusion of solidarity, for experiencing shunyata. There are physical practices, usually strenuous, which create altered states of consciousness. There are the koans of Zen that throw the mind into a hammerlock from which it can escape only by letting go of some of its rigid ways of thinking. There is the curious Tibetan practice called the dream yoga in which you deliberately view waking experience as a dream and thereby contact the activity of creating a world of things out of the mysterious raw material of sensory experience. (The dream yoga is the easiest way I know of to move directly into an altered state of consciousness.)

I am sure that readers of this journal are familiar with most of the practices I have mentioned here, and no doubt with many others as well; my point in reviewing some of the practices of Buddhism is to call attention to their function as techniques of exploration. And they are, of course, meant to be used for a purpose. Buddhism operates from a "principle of uncertainty" no less profound than Heisenberg's: Heisenberg tells us that the act of observation alters that which is observed; Buddhism tells us that the act of observation alters the observer.

Shunyata and Personal Development

"By paying attention to shunyata," says one Buddhist text, "one becomes heedful of the good and wholesome."[13] The Buddhist view is that correctly perceiving the nature of the physical cosmos is a transformative event that has profound consequences for the development of the whole person. The contemporary Tibetan teachers are quite explicit about this. Chogyam Trungpa writes: "The experience of shunyata brings a sense of independence, a sense of freedom . . . . Shunyata provides the basic inspiration for developing the ideal, so to speak, of bodhisattva-like behavior."[14]

Tarthang Tulku has recently written a remarkable — and remarkably difficult — book entitled *Time, Space and Knowledge;* it is both a theoretical exposition of the whole subject of how we order ourselves in the physical universe, and an experiential guide to ways of finding one's way into a different perception of time and space. I would like to quote a fairly long passage from this book, since it gives an excellent statement of the proposition that an incorrect view of the real nature of matter is fundamental to many of our psychological and social problems. Tarthang Tulku writes:

> What we perceive as solid or opaque "things," produced by a given "setting," define by contrast what we perceive as the "space" of that level. So, by attending *only* to the apparently solid things and the contrasting space resulting from one particular "setting," we cannot discover the actual nature of either "existence" or appearance.
>
> Throughout history, we have been maintaining a fixed and limited "focal setting," *without even being aware of doing so.* Yet, although our familiar world seems to depend upon this "setting," if we become able to change the "setting," fantastic new knowledge and appreciation of life can be gained.

The idea of discovering new space may seem at first to be a purely abstract, intellectual endeavor. But in fact it is rooted in the deeply felt need to find an alternative to the sense of restriction and confinement which each of us experiences in our daily lives. This feeling of a lack of space, whether on a personal, psychological level, or at an interpersonal, sociological level, has led to experience of confusion, conflict, imbalance, and general negativity within modern society. We find ourselves setting up strict definitions of territorial boundaries, either as individuals or as larger groups or nations — and great amounts of our energies are utilized in protecting and defending these boundaries. But if we can begin to open our perspective and discover new dimensions of space within our immediate experiences, the anxiety and frustration which results from our sense of limitation will automatically be lessened; and we can increase our ability to relate sensitively and effectively to ourselves, to others, and to the environment.[15]

Some readers may find this easy to understand and accept at least provisionally as theoretical proposition; others may not. I think, initially, it is most important merely to take it as evidence that in the Tibetan Buddhist tradition cosmology and psychology are not separated, that the basic "problem" of life for the unenlightened is as much a way of looking at the physical universe as it is an erroneous conception of the self — or, to be more precise, that thing-centered experience and ego-centered thought are two sides of the same coin.

The Buddhist tradition regards the shunyata experience as of tremendous importance, nothing less than life-transforming, and yet, in a way, refuses to take it too seriously. It is never represented as a bizarre or supernatural experience; it is seeing precisely the world you see already, but in a different way. In the Buddhist view you are already living in that experience, but telling yourself otherwise. "There is no thought, no action which is not substanceless," said the Buddha.[16] Furthermore, numerous texts warn against becoming a true believer, developing an attachment to the concept or to the experience. You merely take in the information it gives you, and move on. There are other experiences beyond shunyata.

Things are in the Saddle

Once we begin to gain some appreciation of the place that shunyata occupies in the Buddhist tradition — as a concept and as an experience, as a way of looking at the physical world and as a way of understanding the human mind and its penchant for reification — we are then in a position to turn around and take a fresh look at Western culture, and to perceive our situation more clearly:

"Things are in the saddle," said Emerson, "And ride mankind."[17] Any thoughtful analysis of the fundamental and recurrent ills of Western society would be likely to include some reference to greed, materialism, attachment, the dehumanizing tendencies of massive social organizations that deal with human beings as things rather than as life processes. We know that these are the source of enormous human misery, yet we are strikingly deficient in insights into the nature of the problem.

We do not, for one thing, really know that we have what amounts to a social paradigm, a socially conditioned and socially enforced world-view concerning physical reality and sensory experience. We assume that in our everyday lives we perceive our physical environment "the way it is," even though modern science, our most respected definer of reality, tells us that is *not* the way it is. We don't know precisely how the thing-centered world-view is learned and maintained in the individual psyche (although we have good reason to suspect that the language is a major factor) and we do not have any concepts in the general culture of an alternative way of perceiving the physical environment — except, as I will mention below, negative concepts. Nor do we understand clearly that such concepts do exist in other cultures; it is an aspect of Buddhism that has been rather consistently misinterpreted.

Lacking a concept of an alternative way of experiencing the physical environment, we naturally do not have any serious body of psychological knowledge — or even much speculation—about the possible connections between such experiences and general mental or emotional well-being. Tarthang Tulku's notion, that our way of experiencing space underlies many of our psychological and political problems, naturally seems a bit far-out. Our only psychological lore in this area has to do with spatial distortions experienced by people in episodes of psychosis or under drugs. More often than not these are reported as frightening or unpleasant — which may be accurate: I suspect that many people in such situations slip into a spontaneous experience of shunyata or a non-Newtonian perception of the physical universe and, lacking the preparation that is provided in such traditions as Buddhism, are terrified by it. We need a more sensitive understanding of such experiences, but — and this is a much taller order — we need to consider the possibility, if we are to make a really serious attempt to hear the message of Buddhism, that the state of mind we call ordinary sanity is itself one in which physical reality is distorted, and that there may be another way of being that is neither psychotic nor hallucinatory, but a quite practical higher sanity.

I have been using the word "we" rather freely, and I assume that readers understand what I mean by it — most of us, the social consensus, the mainstream, the majority. Of course there are people who have by some path — scientific, spiritual, whatever — arrived at a comprehension and a way of living in the world that is different from the social paradigm. But they are a very, very, small minority.

I don't know of any way that such comprehension or experience can be achieved except on an individual basis, one person figuring it out at a time; I don't think Buddhism knows of any way either. For all its wisdom, it is still only a step along the road of human evolution. It is awesome to contemplate what a next step might be, what the world might be like if many or all human beings came to a different way of experiencing the phsyical environment. It is so awesome that it is not easily conceived as a possible historical development — that we might ever find some way to get there from here. The only thing that makes it seem possible at all is the clarity of the message from both ancient Buddhism and modern physics that, whether we know it or not, we are there already and always have been.

References

1. *Open Secrets: A Western Guide to Tibetan Buddhism* (New York: Viking, 1979).

2. Trans. Edward Conze, in Conze *et al* (eds.) *Buddhist Texts Through the Ages* (New York: Harper Torchbooks, 1964), p. 152.

3. *Treasures on the Tibetan Middle Way* (Berkeley: Shambhala, 1973), p. 45.

4. *Psychotherapy East and West* (New York: Pantheon, 1961), p. ix.

5. *Opticks,* quoted in M. P. Crossland (ed.) *The Science of Matter* (Harmondsworth, England: Penguin, 1971), p. 76.

6. *The Tao of Physics* (New York: Bantam, 1977), p. 50.

7. *The Nature of Physical Theory* (New York: Wiley, 1964), p. 21.

8. See *Physics and Philosophy* (New York: Harper & Row, 1962).

9. "Theoretical Physics Must Deal with Thought — Bohm," *Brain/Mind Bulletin,* Sept. 19, 1977, p. 2.

10. *Fragment* no. 81.

11. Translation adapted by author from W. Y. Evans-Wentz, *The Tibetan Book of the Great Liberation* (New York: Oxford), pp. 214-215.

12. For an introduction to this material *see* Herbert V. Guenther, *Philosophy and Psychology in the Abhidharma* (Berkeley: Shambhala, 1976).

13. Gampopa, *The Jewel Ornament of Liberation,* trans. H. V. Guenther, (Berkeley: Shambhala, 1971), p. 224.

14. *The Dawn of Tantra* (with H. V. Guenther), (Berkeley: Shambhala, 1975), p. 34.

15. (Berkeley: Dharma Publishing, 1977), pp.4-5.

16. *Vajrasamadhi Sutra,* trans. Arthur Waley, *Buddhist Texts Through the Ages,* p. 281.

17. *Ode Inscribed to W. H. Channing.*

Walt Anderson, Ph.D. (political science, social psychology) is a former contributing editor of *Human Behavior* magazine and a member of the board of editors of the *Journal of Humanistic Psychology.* He has written many books and articles on politics, psychology, and American culture; his most recent book is *Open Secrets: A Western Introduction to Tibertan Buddhism.* He is currently at work on a book entitled *The God in the Baths* about the Esalen Institute and the origins of the human potential movement.

This article appeared in the 1980 Special Spring issue of the *American Theosophist.*

> 4 <

GROWTH AND BALANCE THROUGH DIALECTICAL MEDITATION
Haridas Chaudhuri

Dialectical meditation is the technique of self-discipline most appropriate to the ideal of balanced and mature personality growth. It is specifically designed to achieve integral self-realization by integrating the seemingly incompatible aspects of personality: the intellectual and the intuitional, the rational and the transrational, the critical, and the mystical.

Dialectical meditation is like the art of gardening in the domain of consciousness. It aims to transform one's total being into a beautiful garden with a thousand flowers in blossom, each with its own unique charm of design, melody of color and thrilling touch of fragrance. But in the maintenance and creation of the garden, the sharpness of the pruning knife and the tenderness of the appreciative hand work together. A beautiful garden needs the judicious use of pesticides and construction of protective fences no less than adequate fertilization and regular watering. Likewise, it needs the full critical evaluation and ruthless rejection of the irrelevant and the incompatible no less than positive concentration and assimilation of the relevant and dedication to the chosen goal.

This form of meditation is the dynamic synthesis of the rational and the transrational, the evolutionary and the transcendental modes of awareness of reality. Such a synthesis alone can serve as the firm foundation for integrated and fruitful living.

Transcendental Consciousness

According to the traditional view, the ultimate goal of meditation is the attainment of transcendental consciousness (turiya). Whereas empirical consciousness consists in perceptual awareness of the phenomenal world of change and relativity, transcendental consciousness is believed to reveal with unerring immediacy the immutable being and eternal perfection of the absolute reality or the ultimate ground of all existence. The absolute or the ultimate has been variously designated as God, Supreme Being, Brahman, Tao, timeless Spirit, eternal Logos, absolute void, indeterminable existence-consciousness-bliss (Saccidananda). The ultimate goal of meditation in the Eastern spiritual tradition is blissful union with the ultimate ground of all existence, no matter by what name it is called.

Unfortunately, more often than not the concept of transcendental consciousness has proved very misleading partly due to the inexactitude of language and partly due to the intellect's proclivity to wishful thinking and misconstruction.

How is the absolute, eternal, and ultimate reality of meditation, related to the phenomenal world of change and relativity? Is the phenomenal world an entirely different kind of order of reality existing in complete separation from, or out of continuity with the absolute? In that case we have an unmitigated dualism of two absolutes separated by a gulf of ignorance.

Is the phenomenal world an inferior, imperfect, and secondary type of reality existing on separation from — and yet in utter dependence upon — the absolute? This also implies a metaphysical dualism militating against the nondual unity and eternal perfection of the absolute.

In order to avoid the consequence of metaphysical dualism some boldly go to the extreme length of declaring the phenomenal world as absolutely unreal or non-existent from the ultimate standpoint, even though it may be real from the standpoint of ignorance (avidya) i.e., the empirical and conventional standpoint. This is, to be sure, a logically perfect sequel to the doctrine of meditation as direct revelation of the eternally perfect absolute. But, alas, logical perfection in the mode of vertical consistency is a sheer abstraction which hovers like a shadow at the opposite extreme to the concrete fullness of life.

It is the doctrine of unreality of the phenomenal world, a logical sequel to the timeless perfection of the absolute of meditation, which has been responsible for the Eastern peoples' lack of progress or comparative backwardness in the phenomenal world due to blissful indifference to the values of time, evolution, and history.

According to integral philosophy — the philosophy that affirms the integral fullness of life and reality — transcendental consciousness *must not* be interpreted as the revelation of any separate, self-existent, absolute and eternally perfect reality. Correct interpretation reveals the true meaning of meditation as a higher perspective — as a penetrative insight into the depth dimension of the same universe which is disclosed to our sensory perception. Our perceptual experience focuses attention upon the endless details, the perishing moments, the disparate segments of the infinitely variegated universe. Meditative intuition, illumination, reveals the nonspatial, nontemporal, undifferentiated, and unmanifest depth dimension of the same universe. This unmanifest depth dimension, when interpreted by different illuminati, under different historical circumstances, gives rise to pragmatically different concepts of the same cosmic whole such as Brahman, Tao, Void, Nothingness, Emptiness, Indeterminable Being, pure existence-consciousness-bliss, and the like. Even though symbols of the same experience, these different metaphysical concepts represent mutually exclusive metaphysical systems of mysticism. This gives rise to dogmatism, mystic claims to absolutism and cognitive monopolism, and consequent divisiveness in global human society.

The mystic's denunciation of the physical and phenomenal world is an indication of the lopsided character of his spiritual realization. Over-exaltation of the mystical experience and the consequent deprecation of the physical-social world justify the mystic in his peace-loving decision for splendid isolation or apathetic aloofness from the creative advance of time and evolution.

On close examination it will be found that the mystic's metaphysical interpretation of the transcendental consciousness as absolute knowledge of eternal perfection commits the fallacy of false superimposition (maya) inspired by wishful speculation and untrained subjectivism. It ignores the fundamental epistemological truth that thought and experience, or intellect and intuition, are inseparably interrelated and interpenetratingly coextensive factors of all human knowledge. The mystic's fallacious absolutism is due to his lack of sufficient training in critical analysis and evaluation alongside of his cultivation through meditation of the intuitive and holistic functions of the psyche.

The mystic affirms on the one hand that the ultimate is absolutely indeterminable and at the same breath characterizes the same ultimate as Being, Non-being, Tao, Void, Emptiness, Nothingness, Divine Darkness. This is evidently a euphoric exercise in self-contradiction. All these awe-inspiring terms, insofar as they are distinctively meaningful, are interpretive categories of thought or intellect. It is as meaningful metaphysical or ontological categories that they have been elaborately developed in their respective systems of philosophy.

Moreover, the mystic's affirmation of the ultimate of meditation either as the only absolute reality or as a higher order of reality in addition to the lower world of perceptual phenomena creates unresolved philosophical problems of thought. An unresolved problem of thought means either hypocritical conduct in society or a schizophrenic behavior pattern. For instance, take the case of a person who is uncertain and undecided regarding the problem of the dualism of God and Mammon, i.e., the conflicting ideals of dedication to truth and unscrupulous pursuit of money. Due to his inner uncertainty, he may develop a hypocritical life style. On Sundays he will go to the church to satisfy his wavering faith in God, the True, the Good and the Beautiful. But during the remaining days of the week he will pour out his whole being into the mad pursuit of money, casting to the four winds all moral scruples and religious injunctions.

Real solutions to the aforesaid problems inherent in the doctrine of absolutely valid knowledge (revelation or spiritual intuition) would consist in the frank recognition of the fact that even the highest religious faith or the purest transcendental consciousness of man is only relatively valid, not absolutely valid knowledge. All knowledge, whether scientific, or religious, or mystical and transcendental, is the interpenetration of thought and experience, reason and intuition, elaborate intellectuality and sensory immediacy. The notion of absolute immediacy and unerring knowledge immanent in religious revelation or mystical intuition is a transcendental illusion of nescience. It is a projection of wishful speculation prompted by unconscious needs of the psyche. It is a false superimposition of maya, the mind's projective mechanism, presenting longed-for possibility as immediately given actuality. In ultimate analysis, it is the essential structure of all human knowledge, in which sensory, imaginative, or intuitive immediacy, rational interpretation, and emotional reaction inseparably interpenetrate.

In order therefore to promote the integral growth of personality as well as the continuous advance of culture and civilization, the practice of meditation should include adequate training of the critical, interpretative, and analytical functions of the intellect as well as cultivation of the holistic, synthetic, appreciative, and penetrative functions of the psyche.

The inherent contradictions and inadequacies of the purely intuitional or devotional approach of meditation drive us then by immanent necessity to a careful consideration of the role of intellect or reason in human self-development.

Dr. Haridas Chaudhuri was a disciple of Sri Aurobindo, the renowned Indian spiritual teacher, and his greatest exponent of *integral yoga*. Chaudhuri was Founder and President of the California Institute of Asian Studies in San Francisco until his death. He also served as President of the Cultural Integration Fellowship, dedicated to the promotion of cultural understanding between East and West. He was the author of four books published by The Theosophical Publishing

House, Wheaton, Illinois: *Integral Yoga; Being, Evolution* and *Immortality; Mastering the Problems of Living;* and *The Evolution of Integral Consciousness.*

This article appeared in the August 1978 issue of the *American Theosophist* under the title "Dialectical Meditation: The Art of Balanced and Matured Growth".

$$\Longrightarrow 5 \Longleftarrow$$

MODERN MEDITATION: CAN A SPIRITUAL DISCIPLINE FOSTER MENTAL HEALTH?
Patricia Carrington

The "meditative mood," a mental state in which the mind drifts, alert yet removed from ordinary sensory interaction with the environment, is familiar to every human being. It is present in any uplifting experience which causes a person to be "carried away," to sense their true self, to feel "at one" and at peace. The formalization of this mood into a *technique* known as "meditation," however, is another matter. It is a way of putting it to use. By means of special disciplines designed to bring about the meditative mood at will and to sustain it indefinitely, humankind has managed to harness this elusive state so that it can be used to achieve goals.

Traditionally these goals have been spiritual in nature, but recently forms of meditation have been devised which can be considered "clinical."[1] These new forms may lead to spiritual fulfillment in an individual so inclined, but this is not their specific aim. They are designed to further the mental and emotional health of the individual and it is these clinical forms of meditation which I will be discussing here. While doing so, however, it is important to keep in mind that there are other valid uses of meditation, not the least among them its traditional use for achieving higher states of consciousness and developing one's inner life.

The clinical forms of meditation were derived by extracting, from the countless forms of meditation available, the elements essential to their therapeutic effect, and from these creating forms of meditation which need not be embedded in any esoteric belief system — a clear advantage for the *clinical* use of these techniques, since it has facilitated their acceptance by medical and mental health practitioners and by academic researchers.

The modern form of meditation most familiar to the West is Transcendental Meditation (TM). TM has firm roots in the Yogic tradition, however, and initiates its trainees by means of a traditional Hindu *puja* ceremony, although the mystical-religious aspects of TM have been disguised in the language of its public relations campaign. The latter has described the technique solely in "scientific" terms and, resultantly, in the early 1970s TM became acceptable to large segments of the non-spiritually inclined (non-*eastern* oriented) public.

The wide dissemination of public information on TM and its benefits resulted in literally hundreds of research studies on this form of meditation. Some of these were of a questionable value from a scientific point of view since they were conducted by researchers with such heightened enthusiasm for meditation that these investigators failed to ensure proper scientific controls. Much research on the TM technique, however, was conducted in leading laboratories by highly respected researchers and carries considerable weight with the scientific community.

Despite the research evidence supporting it, the TM technique is at a disadvantage when it comes to the clinical use of meditation. The time-consuming and expensive personal instruction by TM teachers (at this writing a cost of $200 per individual and $300 per couple), the devout Hindu initiation ceremony it uses and the "secretly" assigned TM mantras, have discouraged the use of TM in clinical settings. Hospitals, medical centers, guidance clinics and private mental health practitioners are not eager to recommend a technique over which they cannot exert personal control and supervision, and the TM organization's continued insistence that to be qualified to exert such control a clinician must spend six months in residence to become a certified TM teacher (or forego the privilege of being able to suggest even minor alterations in the meditation technique, even for clinical reasons) has proven a barrier to acceptance of this modern form of meditation by the medical-psychiatric community.

This can be better understood when we see that it is a distinct advantage for a clinician to recommend a form of meditation which he or she can personally teach or supervise. It not only eliminates undue expense for the client, but permits a sensitive adjustment of the meditation technique to suit the personality and special requirements of the particular patient. This is essential because proper adjustment of the technique can make the difference between its successful use for the promotion of mental health or the unfortunate appearance of meditation "side effect" which may cause a therapeutic setback by paradoxically *increasing* anxiety.[1] In fact, it has become apparent that a complete *training* program in meditation, geared to each individual's unique needs, is essential to its successful use in any mental health setting.

Fortunately, there are now forms of meditation available for clinical use which have the required flexibility for this purpose. Dr. Herbert Benson of Harvard Medical School devised a simple form of breathing meditation (Respiratory One Method, or ROM) which has been used clinically to elicit what he terms the "relaxation response."[2] ROM is taught in two pages of written instruction (in Benson's book) or by means of roughly five minutes of verbal directions.

Carrington[3] has developed a one-week tape-recorded training program in a modern form of mantra meditation, Clinically Standardized Meditation (or CSM), which was derived from ancient Indian sources. The CSM method is designed to be used by psychotherapists and other mental health practitioners, or by those members of the general public who wish to follow a complete instructional system in meditation which is specifically geared to individual differences. The method is taught through three cassette recordings and an accompanying programmed instruction test. In clinical settings it is usually supervised by medical or psychiatric personnel, but for trainees *not* undergoing any form of treatment, it is a self-instructional system.

As modern westernized forms of meditation are beginning to be used in settings never before considered as likely places for meditation — for example, in industry and medicine — we find that these simple techniques, which limit stimulus input and center attention upon some constant object of focus (a mentally repeated sound, the breath, etc.) are extremely easy for the average westerner to learn. They are also sufficiently pleasant to keep the habit of meditating going on a fairly regular basis. The dropout rate thus appears to be no greater for meditation than it is for any other major self-help program. In a recent research study conducted at the New York Telephone Company,[4] for example, 81% of the trainees who had learned CSM were found to be still practicing it at the end of the study (5½ months later).

Let us look at the clinical benefits of meditation and how it can be used to foster mental health:

The Physiology of Meditation

Meditation represents a physiological state showing some of the qualities of both sleep and wakefulness, yet distinct from either. When laboratory measurements have been taken on meditating subjects, the electro-physiological records show a quieting down of body and mind which in many ways is similar to that of the deepest sleep stages. Oxygen consumption typically drops in a completely natural manner during a twenty-minute period of meditation to a degree usually found to be the case only after six or seven hours of sleep.[5] Heart and respiration rates also slow down normally at this time and the ability of the skin to conduct electrical current (generally considered to be an indication of anxiety) both decreases and stabilizes during meditation.[6] Doctors Keith Wallace and Herbert Benson have thus called the meditative state "hypometabolic," meaning that during meditation the metabolism of the body becomes slower and more quiet, a pattern physiologically opposite to the body's "alarm: or fight-or-flight" response. At the same time, meditation involves an *active* process of attention — although reducing physiological arousal, it leaves mental alertness undiminished.[7] In this respect, meditation is strikingly different from sleep, a fact which may account for some of its unique benefits.

Over the past few years a growing number of research studies have documented a number of "carry-over" effects of meditation on the lives of those who practice, effects which make this technique valuable as an aid to psychotherapy. Some of the most important are here presented:

Stress Reduction

Much research suggests that meditation can reduce the amount of stress which people experience. In one recent experiment performed in England, investigators attempted to find out whether individuals who practiced meditation would show less reaction to stressful stimulation than a group of matched control subjects. All subjects were placed in a laboratory and exposed to loud, grating sounds, the kind that "set your teeth on edge." While the nonmeditators tended to tense up during the experiment, the meditators showed only very few arousal or "alarm" reactions — most of the time they were quietly relaxed.[8]

In another study, meditators and nonmeditators were shown a film depicting a grisly woodshop accident.[9] This film has been used as a stimulus in much research on stress and never fails to generate heightened alarm reactions in those who view it. Yet both the physiological research and the reports of the subjects themselves indicated that the meditators tolerated the film with less stress than did the nonmeditators. These findings and the results of other investigations suggest that meditators may actually develop a degree of immunity to stress.

Improvement in Stress-Related Illnesses

Every research study conducted so far where the effects of meditation on anxiety have been measured has shown anxiety to be sharply reduced in a majority of people after they commenced meditation. Because of this, meditation has a strong, positive effect on many stress-related illnesses and medical facilities are now beginning to use meditation along with regular medical treatment for these illnesses. A series of studies on the use of meditation for the normalizing of blood pressure, for example, report a reliable decrease in blood pressure in a substantial number of people who have learned meditation.[10] Other studies have shown meditation to be useful in the treatment of tension headaches,[11] bronchial asthma,[12] and heart disease,[13] as well as other stress-related illnesses.

Most patients who respond to meditation with improvement of a medical condition must keep on meditating regularly to maintain their gains, however. In such cases meditation is like a change of diet which eliminates symptoms only as long as the diet is faithfully followed.

Increased Coping Ability

Greater alertness is a frequently documented benefit of meditation. People who are meditating regularly tend to handle tasks in a more efficient manner, and this increased coping ability seen in meditators is quite different from that brought about by taking a tranquilizing drug. Relaxation resulting from drugs tends to slow a person down. By contrast, groups of meditators have been shown to react faster on visual tasks than nonmeditators,[14] to discriminate more accurately between different sounds,[15] and to get better scores on tests of manual dexterity.[16] In other words, meditation seems to *increase* energy.

Greater Productivity

Another frequently reported benefit of meditation is an increase in productivity. When organizational psychologist Dr. David Frew investigated the effects of meditation on 500 men and women in business,[17] he found that job satisfaction increased; work performance improved; turnover potential was reduced (less tendency to want to switch companies); relationships with supervisors improved; and relationships with coworkers improved.

43

A number of research studies have also shown meditators to have a freer flow of ideas than nonmeditators,[18] in certain instances disabling blocks to creativity have dissolved completely after a person commenced meditation,[1] and meditators may feel greatly increased energy in general. With clients undergoing psychotherapy, this freeing of energy is frequently reflected in the greater ease with which the client is able to approach difficult material during his or her psychotherapy session and the rapidity with which he is able to reach innovative solutions to problems.

Control of Addictions

Meditation often helps meditators gain control over troubling addictions. In one study, researchers found that the number of marijuana users was reduced to nearly one-third the original amount among meditators, while the figures for nonmeditators remained approximately the same over an identical period of time.[19]

When these same investigators studied cigarette smokers, they found that 71% of those who have practiced meditation *for more than two years* reported a significant decrease in their use of cigarettes, and 57% had totally stopped smoking by that time, while at the end of a similar period, nonmeditators were smoking as heavily as before.[20]

Consumption of alcohol was affected by meditation, too. Of those meditators who had been meditating regularly for more than two years, 40% reported that they had stopped drinking either beer or wine, while none of the nonmeditators had stopped. After three years of meditation the figures were even higher—60% of the meditators had now stopped drinking beer and wine. In addition, 54% of this last group (as against 1% of the nonmeditating group) had also stopped drinking hard liquor.[21]

These and other studies suggest that meditation can be effective in combating addictions — providing that a person stays with the meditation for a sufficient period of time. There seems to be a clearcut relationship between the amount of time people have spent meditating and their ability to cut down on drugs, cigarettes or alcohol — the longer, the better.

On a clinical level, I have observed several of my patients lose interest in heavy use of marijuana after commencing meditation; two patients bring incipient drinking problems under control; two patients stop smoking; and two (non-obese) patients spontaneously regulate their need for food intake after commencing meditation. My clients with severe obesity problems have not shown any lessening of their compulsive eating after starting meditation and shown no weight loss — they did, however, benefit from the practice in other respects.

Improvement of Sleep

Insomnia tends to respond extremely well to meditation. In one study, after commencing meditation, subjects who had regularly lain awake for one and a quarter hours each night before falling asleep now typically fell asleep within fifteen minutes after lying down in bed.[22] A study from a different laboratory has shown that such improvement in sleep habits continues and, in fact, may be even greater after subjects have been meditating for six months.[23]

Meditation can also affect the entire way a person experiences life — indirectly this may be one of its most important contributions to preventive medicine. It is well-known that the happier one is, the less apt one is to contract illness.

Here are some of the changes in attitude that can be brought about by meditation:

Greater Self-Acceptance

Many people conduct an inner dialogue in which they repeatedly criticize themselves for not behaving "properly" or not doing things "well enough." A frequent change resulting from meditation is the toning down or elimination of this kind of self-criticism. Meditators tend to become more patient and understanding with themselves and less apt to indulge in unjustified self-blame.[24]

As a result they may develop a greater tolerance for other people. One of the most frequent comments of friends and families of meditators is that they are now much easier to get along with, less irritable and more understanding of those around them.[24]

More Inner Independence

Many meditators report a sharp increase in "inner in-dependence." They may find that they can now identify their own opinions and feelings more easily, sense their personal "rights" in situations where formerly they may have been unaware of them, and withstand social pressures better without abandoning their own opinions.[25] As a consequence, they may become more decisive and better able to express opinions more openly and can disagree with others more effectively and demand their own rights in situations where formerly they would have capitulated.

Mood Changes

Meditators frequently find that their moods are lighter as well as more stable after commencing meditation and, as a consequence, experience a renewed sense of well-being. Although outer circumstances often remain unchanged, their lives often seem happier and more fulfilling than before.[26]

Decreased Self-Blame

Many clinicians working with meditating patients, myself included, have noticed a tendency toward self-recrimination become remarkably lessened in these patients after they commenced meditating. This result is both stress-reducing and an obvious advantage for psychotherapy, since it permits formerly threatening material to be faced openly in the counseling situation and handled with comparative ease.

More Available Affect

Clients who have commenced meditating frequently report that they not only experience lessened anxiety, but that they also experience stronger feelings of pleasure, sadness, anger, love, or other emotions — feelings which they may previously have suppressed. This emotional release may occur *during* a meditation session, or it may occur outside of such a session at anytime during the day, seemingly with little connection to meditation other than the fact that this is an unaccustomed experience for the person who has it.

Because meditation increases the ease with which people can experience genuine emotion, it is often useful to ask the patient to meditate immediately before coming to a psychotherapy session. I have found that post-meditation therapy sessions tend to be more productive, with patients more in touch with their own feelings and better able to express what is truly troubling them than when they have not recently meditated.

Another clinical use of meditation is when progress *during* a psychotherapy session is blocked. When a patient is unable to deal meaningfully with a problem, seeming to circle around the really important issues (no matter how skillfully the psychotherapist may attempt to intervene), my colleagues and I have found an extraordinarily useful maneuver to be to suggest to the patient that patient and therapist meditate *together* for about ten minutes *during* the therapy session. After having meditated in this manner the rapport between therapist and patient is usually deep, with the patient relaxed, thoughtful and in touch with his or her feelings. There is an attunement that occurs when therapist and patient have joined together in the nonverbal sharing of meditation. I have never known this experience to fail to bring myself and my patient together in a more mutual sharing of the psychotherapy, with both its problems and solutions.

Meditation may also assist the recovery of memories during psychotherapy. Dr. Bernard Glueck[27] has indicated that the reduced level of anxiety which so often results from meditation seems to "facilitate entry into consciousness of previously repressed anxiety-laden material" and I have seen some dramatic instances of traumatic, repressed memories which were recovered during a meditation session. These have been reported in detail elsewhere, but it is important to note that if these memories had occurred during meditation to a person who did not happen to be undergoing psychotherapy at the time, the chances are that the individual concerned might well have abandoned the practice of meditation because of the anxiety of having to face hitherto unrecognized and potentially threatening aspects of his own self. This is evidence of another trend that many of us have noticed — that a combination of psychotherapy and meditation, for purposes of handling troubling emotional problems, is frequently more effective than either of these interventions used alone.

To summarize, the most common situations where meditation has been shown to be useful are as follows:

- Persistent tension and anxiety
- Stress-related illnesses (high blood pressure, bronchial asthma, tension headaches, others)
- Chronic fatigue
- Insomnia
- Chronic pain
- Overuse of "soft" drugs, alcohol or tobacco
- Tendency toward excessive self-blame
- Irritability
- Moderate depression (meditation is not useful for for severe depressions)
- Difficulty in asserting oneself
- Uncontrolled grief persisting longer than normal
- Difficulty in separating from another person when necessary; anxiety at being alone
- Difficulty in experiencing one's own deeper feelings (or in expressing them)
- Blocked productivity or creativity

In addition to handling problems, meditation can be useful clinically because it contributes to the self-development and personal growth of the patient. Some common ways are:

- Improving physical coordination and speed in athletics
- Increasing job proficiency
- Improving capacity for efficient learning and study
- Increasing capacity to relate to others with openness and warmth
- Increasing enjoyment of oneself and a sense of harmony with life

Reasons for Meditation's Clinical Effects

It is well-known that regularly or rhythmically repeated sounds and movements are soothing. For example, a parent will often pick up an agitated baby and rock it with an intuitive awareness of the soothing effects that these rhythmic actions have on the child. For this reason the tranquilizing properties of rhythm may be a key to some of meditation's effects, for rhythm is a basic component of meditation. The rhythm of the "mantra" as it is being repeated is the most obvious, but there are also subtle rhythms of breathing and heartbeat that may come sharply into awareness during the inner stillness of *any* type of meditation. Some people have likened the experience of meditating to being rocked dreamily "as though one were in a small boat bobbing at anchor in a gentle sea." The feeling of well-being that typically results from meditation may, in part at least, be related to its rhythmical nature.

Meditation can also be viewed as an erasing or "desensitizing" procedure. When thoughts or images about the stresses of ordinary life pass through our minds in this deeply relaxed and peaceful state they may be partially neutralized. Such a process, regularly repeated, may attune our nervous system to being less easily aroused by stress.

In addition to such technical explanations, there are the obvious practical benefits of interrupting one's life periodically to become inwardly still. As psychologist Dr. Robert Woolfolk points out:

> At the very least, meditation can give the mind a rest — a brief vacation from stress and worry, one that requires neither a travel agent nor days free from the responsibilities of work or family. When focusing all attention upon a mantra or meditative object, one cannot simultaneously be paying attention to stressful events or thoughts . . . . It is almost as though meditation allows us to temporarily shut down those information-processing mechanisms of the brain that are ultimately responsible for producing stress. This short vacation from stress revitalizes our coping abilities, giving us a more balanced outlook and increased energy for dealing with whatever difficulties we are faced with.
> *Stress, Sanity, and Survival,* pp. 170-171[28]

Caution in the use of Meditation

While helpful to many people, meditation is not a panacea. There are difficulties which can occur if meditation is used incorrectly, the reason why expert training in the handling of medication, with adjustment of the technique to suit individual requirements, is essential to obtain good therapeutic results. Some of the stumbling blocks the clinician runs into when using meditation for emotional problems are as follows:

1. An occasional person may be hypersensitive to meditation so that much shorter sessions than the average are needed. Such people may not be able to tolerate the usual fifteen to twenty minutes sessions prescribed, say, by such methods as TM. They may require drastic reductions in meditation-time before they can benefit from their technique. Most problems of this sort which I have observed have been successfully overcome by careful adjustment of the meditation-time to suit the individual's needs. Such handling requires a systematic method for making such an adjustment and should be part of every responsible training program.

2. *Overmeditation* can be dangerous. On the theory that "if one pill makes me feel better, taking the whole bottle should make me feel exceptionally well!" some people may decide to meditate three or four hours (or more!) per day instead of the prescribed ten to twenty minutes only once or twice a day. Just as with a tonic or medicine, meditation may cease to have beneficial effects if taken in too heavy doses and be detrimental instead. The technique should always be practiced in moderation with the meditator following instructions given in a reliable meditation training program.

3. Even normal amounts of meditation can produce temporary discomforts. Mild discomforts which are occasionally reported by some meditators are normal occurrences which I have termed "tension release side effects." I consider them a useful part of the meditative process, serving to release tension. However, meditators experiencing such side effects without having been informed about them may be either alarmed or unnecessarily discouraged. Such people need to be taught how to handle these temporary annoyances, another reason why thorough training in the *management* of meditation is essential.

Limitations of Meditation in Clinical Practice

Like all other techniques used to effect personality change, meditation has its limitations. The inevitable dropout rate is the least of these since *some* patients drop out of all programs designed to assist them, whether these programs be weight control groups, exercise regimes, smoke-ending programs or even psychotherapy. A potentially serious clinical problem, however, is the rapidity with which certain personality changes occur in meditators and the fact that meditation may bring about behavior changes which do not fit in comfortably with the lifestyle or defensive system of the patient.

When even positive changes occur before a groundwork for them has been laid (by readjustment of the patient's value system) an impasse may occur which is then resolved in one of two ways:

(1) The pathological value system is altered to incorporate the new attitude brought about by meditation; or

(2) The process of meditation is abandoned.

It is often crucial (in determining which choice is made) that the patient have recourse to psychotherapy for working through the difficulties involved. This may determine whether or not this particular person will continue with meditation and use it to effect a basic change in lifestyle, or whether he or she will run from it.

Here are some of the ways that modern forms of meditation can threaten a patient's pathological lifestyle:

1. Meditation can foster a healthy self-assertion which clashes with neurotic needs to be self-effacing, a "martyr" and overly submissive. Such traits are usually deep-seated ones, so that some meditators who have lived all their lives "in the shadows," so to speak, can be startled, even frightened, to find themselves becoming more bold and assertive. However, with the encouragement of an understanding counselor or psychotherapist, they may realize why, in the first place, they had to be so self-effacing and so may gain courage to benefit considerably from meditation.

2. Meditation can foster feelings of well-being and optimism which threaten a lifetime pattern of being depressed or "long-suffering." Sometimes the patient is experiencing unconscious *gains* in the role of being a failure and may be reluctant to relinquish such a role, although they do not realize that this is the case. The result may be that they actually give up meditation instead, *unless* the problem is handled by insight into this difficulty, arrived at during the course of psychotherapy.

3. Pleasurable feelings encountered during or following meditation may cause anxiety in their own right. Our civilization is, in many ways, dominated by the Puritan ethic, so that spending time with oneself, allowing oneself to enjoy leisure, or just plain doing something which is considered "a waste of time" in our culture may cause so much guilt that such persons will abandon the practice of meditation entirely unless they have recourse to professional help to enable them to understand their irrational concerns and modify their values.

4. Meditation may bring an easing of life-pace which can be threatening to one who has a very fast-paced, high-pressured lifestyle used as defense against unacceptable feelings, or perhaps in the service of an overpowering drive for power, achievement, or control. Under such conditions, obviously the underlying problem is the person's lifestyle and value system and meditation can only be fitted into such a life when the hidden anxieties or ambitions are unearthed and dealt with.

In all the above instances the patients concerned may simply refuse to learn meditation, or they may learn it but quickly discontinue it, unless the underlying conflict is handled in psychotherapy. On the other hand, patients' negative reactions to meditation can be extremely fruitful material to work on in their psychotherapy sessions, since discussion of the meditation-related problem often unmasks self-defeating aspects of a neurotic process which can now, for the first time, be handled in a constructive fashion.

Of course such complications do not by any means occur in *all* meditating patients. Sometimes the meditation assists the course of therapy in such a straightforward fashion that there is little, if any, necessity to investigate the patient's reactions to it. A number of healthy persons certainly appear to benefit from meditation without difficulties of any sort, and the same is true of a number of patients undergoing psychotherapy.

Conclusions

Modern forms of meditation seem to be clearly promising as aids to psychotherapy, provided the meditation is accompanied by insight into any resistance to it which may arise as a function of the patient's pre-existing problems, and also provided that careful and complete training in meditation is given patients and that the technique is adjusted to suit their clinical needs.

It is therefore indeed gratifying to find that more and more psychotherapists are making use of meditation with their patients and also using it effectively for themselves. Our clinical observations have shown that meditating psychotherapists tend to be more open and accepting of the negative reactions that patients may express during their therapeutic hour; that they tend to become more sensitively aware of symbolic material (such as dreams); and that these therapists become more empathic and openly accepting of their patients after starting the practice of meditation.[28] These benefits alone suggest that modern forms of meditation can be utilized very effectively in psychotherapeutic settings, as well as incorporated into the training which clinicians undergo in order to become effective therapists. It is my hope that such developments will continue with the same momentum and that we will see many more therapeutic applications of meditation in the 1980s. It may well be, in fact, that this ancient spiritual discipline will play a significant, perhaps even a central role in the healing of the modern human psyche.

References

1. P. Carrington, *Freedom in Meditation* (New York: Doubleday), 1977.

2. H. Benson, *The Relaxation Response* (New York: William Morrow), 1975.

3. P. Carrington, *Learning to Meditate: A Self-Regulated Course in Clinically Standardized Meditation* (Kendall Park, NJ: Pace Educational Systems), 1978.

4. P. Carrington, "The Use of Meditation-Relaxation Techniques for the Management of Stress in Working Population." Paper presented at the Annual Meeting of the Association for the Advancement of Behavior Therapy, San Francisco, Dec. 14, 1979.

5. R. K. Wallace and H. Benson, "The Psychology of Meditation," *Scientific American,* vol. 226, 1972, pp. 84-90.

6. D. W. Orme-Johnson, "Automatic Stability and Transcendental Meditation," *Psychosomatic Medicine,* vol. 35, 1973, pp. 341-349.

7. R. K. Wallace, H. Benson and A. F. Wilson, "A Wakeful Hypometabolic State," *American Journal of Physiology,* vol. 221, 1971, pp. 795-799.

8. D. Daniels, Personal communication cited in P. Carrington, *Freedom in Meditation* (New York: Doubleday/Anchor Press), 1977, pp. 60-61.

9. J. D. Goleman and G. E. Schwartz, "Meditation as an Intervention in Stress Reactivity," *Journal of Consulting and Clinical Psychology,* vol. 44, 1976, pp. 456-466.

10. H. Benson and R. K. Wallace, "Decreased Blood Pressure in Hypertensive Subjects who Practiced Meditation," *Circulation,* Supplement II to vols. 45 and 46, 1972, p. 516.

11. P. Carrington, *op. cit.* 1977, pp. 251-253.

12. R. W. Honsberger and A. F. Wilson, "Transcendental Meditation in Treating Asthma," *Respiratory Therapy: The Journal of Inhalation Technology,* vol. 3, 1973, pp. 79-80.

13. J. W. Zamarra, I. Besseghini, and S. Wittenberg, "The Effects of the Transcendental Meditation Program on the Exercise Performance of Patients with Angina Pectoris," in D. W. Orme-Johnson and J. T. Farrow (eds.), *Scientific Research on the Transcendental Meditation Program,* vol. I (Livingston Manor, N.Y., Maharishi European Research University Press), 1978, pp. 331-334.

14. S. Appelle and L. E. Oswald, "Simple Reaction Time as a Function of Alertness and Prior Mental Activity," *Perceptual and Motor Skills,* vol. 38, 1974, 1263-1268.

15. M. Pirot, "The Effects of the Transcendental Meditation Technique Upon Auditory Discrimination," in D. W. Orme-Johnson and J. T. Farrow (eds.), *op. cit,* 1978, pp. 331-334.

16. A. G. P. Rimol, "The Transcendental Meditation Technique and its Effects on Sensory-Motor Performance," *Ibid,* pp. 326-330.

17 D. Frew, *Management of Stress* (Chicago: Nelson-Hall), 1977.

18. M. Hines, "Meditation and Creativity: A Pilot Study," Senior Thesis, Princeton University, 1970.

19. M. Shafii, R. A. Lavely, and R. D. Jaffe, "Meditation and Marijuana," *American Journal of Psychiatry,* vol. 131, 1974,00. 60-63.

20. M. Shafii, "Smoking Following Meditation," Unpublished Paper, Department of Psychiatry, University of Michigan Medical School, Ann Arbor, Michigan, 1973.

21. M. Shafii, R. A. Lavely, and R. Jaffe, "Meditation and the Prevention of Alcohol Abuse," *American Journal of Psychiatry,* vol. 132, 1975, pp. 942-945.

22. D. E. Miskiman, "Long-Term Effects of the Transcendental Meditation Program in the Treatment of Insomnia," D. W. Orme-Johnson and J. T. Farrow (eds.), *op. cit.,* 1978, p. 299.

23. R. L. Woolfolk et al, "Meditation Training as a Treatment for Insomnia," *Behavior Therapy,* vol. 7, 1976, pp. 359-365.

24. P. Carrington and H. S. Ephron, "Meditation as an Adjunct to Psychotherapy," in S. Arieti (ed.), *New Dimensions in Psychiatry: A World View* (New York: John Wiley & Sons), 1975, pp. 262-291.

25. K. R. Pelletier, "The Effects of the Transcendental Meditation Program on Perceptual Style: Increased Field Independence," Paper Presented at annual meeting of the Western Psychological Association, San Francisco, April 25-28, 1974.

26. P. Carrington and H. S. Ephron, "Clinical Use of Meditation," in J. H. Masserman (ed.), *Current Psychiatric Therapies,* vol. 15 (New York: Grune and Stratton), 1975, pp. 101-108.

27. B. Glueck, as quoted in the *Hartford Courant,* May 27, 1973, p. 6.

28. R. L. Woolfolk and F. C. Richard, *Stress, Sanity, and Survival* (New York: Sovereign Books), 1978.

29. P. Carrington and H. S. Ephron, "Meditation and Psychoanalysis," *Journal of the American Academy of Psychoanalysis,* vol. 3, 1975, pp. 43-57.

Patricia Carrington, Ph.D., is a clinical psychologist and lecturer in the Department of Psychology at Princeton University. She has published numerous articles on the new experimental studies of sleep and dreaming, and her work on the use of meditation as an adjunct to psychotherapy is a landmark in this area. Dr. Carrington is the author of the book *Freedom in Meditation* which deals with the use of the modern forms of meditation in the field of mental health. She is presently Administrative Consultant to the Stress Management Program at New York Telephone.

This article appeared in the Special Spring issue, 1980 of *The American Theosophist.*

>6<

WORKING WITH EMOTION: WESTERN AND EASTERN APPROACHES
John Welwood

Because emotion is our most common experience of being moved and taken over by forces seemingly beyond our control, it is one of the most confusing and challenging events in many people's lives. A common tendency in our culture is to treat emotional energy with suspicion or contempt, as alien, "other," separate from us. The "passions," as this energy has often been called, have been viewed as our "lower nature," from Plato onward. Thus we have generally failed to discover how emotion can actually serve as a powerful teacher. Insofar as the vivid energy of emotion intensifies our experience it can expose various fixations of mind and psychological blockages. Emotions may help wake us up to what is happening in our lives. They indicate where we most need to work on ourselves to become more balanced and integrated. And, since they are

---

expressions of our own life energy, experiencing them in a direct and mindful way can help us to feel ourselves more deeply.

The subject of emotion is one of the most confused chapters in modern psychology, in that few psychologists agree about what emotion signifies or even about what words to use in examining it. Anyone wishing to learn about emotion from the literature of Western psychology finds a bewildering array of theories about what it is, how it arises, and how to deal with it in one's life. James Hillman, at the end of an exhaustive study of emotion, concluded that "no matter how thoroughly amplified, the problem of emotion . . . remains perennial and its solution ineffable."[1]

But perhaps it is the dualistic way in which emotion has been thought about that has made it such a difficult problem in Western psychology. The emotions have often been associated with instinctual drives and reactions to them (as by Freud) or with purely physiological response patterns (as by William James). Viewing the source of the passions, as Freud did, as an "it" (translated in English as "id") — "a primitive chaos, a cauldron of seething excitement,"[2] makes it more difficult to befriend emotions and accept them as part of oneself. Thus Western psychology has reinforced the widespread view of emotions as fundamentally alien and "other." For example, Jung states that

> . . . . an emotion is the intrusion of an unconscious personality . . . To the primitive mind, a man who is seized by a strong emotion is possessed by a devil or a spirit; and our language still expresses the same idea, at least metaphorically. There is much to be said in favor of this point of view.[3]

According to James Hillman, a follower of Jung's, "our psychological afflictions and emotions too are not truly ours. They come and go . . . by factors independent of our potency."[4] This view of emotions as primitive and alien is a classic Western way of separating ourselves from them. And it is in sharp contrast to the view of Eastern psychologies, which understand that it is precisely this alienation from emotions that causes them to be domineering and uncontrollable.

If we closely examine what emotions consist of, we actually find that it is not emotional energy per se that is alien and confusing. Rather, emotional energy accentuates any inner confusion and fragmentation that already exists. In particular, emotional energy can intensify the ways our thoughts and fantasies rule and compel us. This compulsion may at times become all-encompassing and all-consuming, so that we are "beside ourselves" or act recklessly.

Viewing emotional energy as alien leads us to deal with it by trying to get rid of it. On the one hand, we may think that the solution to emotion is to get it out of our system — by acting it out impulsively. On the other hand, we might try to suppress or subdue our emotions because they seem so threatening or dangerous. However, both these strategies only lead to further confusion because they neither relate to emotion directly nor allow us to experience what it is. Thus these strategies can be quite aggressive, either toward others or toward ourselves. And they prevent us from discovering how emotion may actually become a vehicle for connecting with ourselves.

How then can we understand and relate to emotions in a direct way? How can we befriend them and accept them as part of ourselves? How can we utilize their potent energy to wake us up from our fixed habits of mind?

Clarifying Terms

Loose and inconsistent use of terms have clouded the subject of emotion in Western psychology. The word "feeling" has been used to refer to a whole spectrum of different kinds of awareness, from vague intuitions ("I feel he may not like me") to intense emotions ("I feel rage"). To avoid this confusion, this spectrum as a whole can be called *felt energy*. And the term "feeling" can be used more precisely to refer to *specific* bodily felt responses to life situations. To begin work with emotions constructively, it is important to see first of all what is involved in this spectrum of felt energy.

A Starting Point: Basic Aliveness

If feeling and emotions are expressions of being alive, we need to understand what this basic aliveness is. Aliveness is our most fundamental experience of ourselves — being present to life at this moment with an open receptivity, which, like a mirror, generously reflects whatever appears in front of it. Though we may often be alienated from this basic aliveness, it is not inherently like "the it" which Freud called "an obscure, inaccessible part of our personality." Rather, it is our most intimate experience of all.

Biologist Rene Dubos equates this sense of aliveness with a fundamental *joie de vivre,* a sense of the wholesomeness of being awake to life, despite all the ups and dows of circumstance:

> About the experience of life, most people are under the illusion that they can be happy only if something especially good happens...Oddly enough, there is only one phrase I know to express that life is good per se, that just being alive is good. Whenever one wants to say that, one uses the French expression — in all languages: one speaks of *joie de vivre. Joie de vivre* simply means that just being alive is an extraordinary experience. It is perhaps the greatest . . . experience one can have. The quality of that experience anyone can see by watching a young child or a young animal playing in the spring. It is totally immaterial what goes on, except for the fact that one is alive. It does not mean that you are very happy with the way you live; you can even be suffering. you can have lots of trouble, but just being alive is a quality per se.[5]

This basic aliveness also has qualities of tenderness and gentleness. Because our fundamental nature is openness and receptivity to the world, we are not only highly sensitive creatures, but also quite vulnerable. Our senses and the intricate workings of the brain and nervous system are geared toward *letting the world in.* Thus we have feeling.

Like water, which is the cradle of life as well as a universal element in all living tissues, our aliveness is both the source of feelings, and contained within them. Like the earth, aliveness surrounds us on all sides, while feeling is something that grows out of this basic ground. Like air, which when breathed into the lungs quickens the whole body with a fresh source of energy, it is the open space in the heart of feelings which keeps them from ever becoming fixed or solid. And it is like fire in its intensity and its warmth. Connecting with this basic sense of aliveness, in which lies our basic sanity and health, is more than what some psychologists have called "getting in touch with our feelings." It is discovering ourselves in our most basic sensitivity, from which all emotions and feelings arise.

Felt Meaning

Every life situation usually means something more to us than the specific feelings and emotions it may give rise to. This "something more" is sensed holistically in terms of "felt meanings." "Felt meanings are a wider sense of things than our usual feelings and emotions, which can lead to new ways of understanding our life situations.

For instance, my feeling of irritation with someone contains many felt meanings enfolded together as a whole. My irritation is familiar, but the particular felt meanings underlying *this particular irritation* are still quite unfamiliar. If I attend to my bodily felt sense of this irritation, I can unfold and articulate some of these felt meanings. ("Let's see — my irritation has something to do with feeling ignored by you, which makes me feel helpless, powerless . . . . And that brings up all this outrage . . . . But that's not the main thing really, it's more that I really *do* want to connect with you, even though you will not recognize me . . . because I do care about you . . ."). Before I attended to them and tried to articulate them, these meanings were felt in a vague background way.

My feeling is thus not only the familiar something I can focus on, but also expresses wider patterns in my life, connected with my ongoing sense of many other past and present situations as well. These multiple relationships, felt holistically, make up a sense of rich possibilities in any given moment.

These potentials exist embryonically underneath our more familiar patterns of feeling and emotional response. One body of research suggests that being in contact with this wider context of felt meaning is the basis of personality change in psychotherapy, and a major source of creative decision-making.[6]

Feeling

Feelings are more recognizable than felt meanings. Even an indescribable feeling is felt as a particular "something." We can sense *that* it is even if we do not know *what* it is. Although in one sense feelings are "inside" us, in that they are felt in the body, they always reflect our relationship with the world. This means that when we feel something, it is not just some isolated event happening inside us, but may be a valuable clue or message about our life at that moment.

Emotion

Emotion is an intense form of feeling. Whereas feeling can be fairly mild or vague, emotion is extremely strong and specific. A *feeling* of fear may lurk in the background of the mind without a specific object, whereas an *emotion* of fear or terror is an unmistakable reaction to something very specific.

The Spectrum of Felt Energy

Figure 1 illustrates the relation of felt meaning, feeling, and emotion:

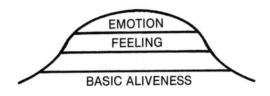

Figure 1. The Spectrum of Felt Energy

At bottom, our nature is aliveness, open to the world. This aliveness is unconditional; it does not depend on feeling good or bad. It is a global sensitivity which, as the world affects us, takes on the form of feeling and emotion.

Felt meaning is an intermediary state between this pure aliveness and specific feelings. Felt meanings are our inward sense of how we relate to particular situations, how we react to this or that about our lives.

Feelings are a combination of basic aliveness and felt meaning. For example, say I move into a new house and am irritated by the traffic noise I discover in the street outside. My feeling of irritation is a mix of: 1) my basic sensitivity, with 2) felt meanings — my sense of the kind of environment I like to live in, how much I can tolerate living in a less than ideal environment, why quiet is important to me, my expectation that this neighborhood would not be noisy, and so on.

Emotion is the further development of feeling, from irritation, say, to angry outrage when the city sanitation engineers start tearing up the street outside with jackhammers. At each successive level of the spectrum, felt energy becomes more channelled and narrowed down, less global and open. If we imagine that Figure 1 is a volcano, we can see that as the energy gets closer to the top, and narrowed into a more condensed form, it takes on greater urgency, pressure, and potential explosiveness. Deep in the ground the molten lava has room to circulate freely, but as it becomes channelled, the force and pressure threaten to erupt. Emotion is thus an intense bodily energy which is about to blow the lid off things, shoot forth into the world. It is this channelling of a larger energy and the pressure this creates that makes many strong emotions rather painful to feel. (Even intense ecstatic emotions can be somewhat stressful, which is why people often cry when they are overjoyed.) They seem almost too much to handle.

The Intensification of Emotion

How is it that feelings develop into the intense emotions that dominate us with their powerful energy?

Contained in my feelings is the tender quality of my basic aliveness, which I would often rather not face. In moving

away from experiencing this aliveness directly, I choose instead to think about my sadness. This gives rise to sad "story-
lines," composed of thoughts and images, memories, projec-
tions into the future, dialogue with myself about my life. But
the more I entertain and mull over these sad thoughts and fantasies, the further they reinforce my sadness, giving new fuel
to it, locking me further into it. And the sadder I become, the
more sad story-lines arise — a vicious circle. This sub-
conscious mulling serves as a catalyst that intensifies the feeling. Emotion develops as this thought/feeling cycle works
itself up into a peak, generating further pressure — I may start
to cry or be overcome by grief and despair. Such phrases as
"out of one's senses" or "swept away" express this driving,
consuming quality of emotion.

Emotional upsurge is like a fire kindled by the cycle of
thoughts intensifying feelings, which in turn give rise to further thoughts, and so on. ("I'm so mad! Why did he do this to
me? I deserve better. I'm going to teach him . . ."). Insofar as
emotions are bound up with these story-lines, they are at once
remove from the present moment, and thus cloud our ability
to see clearly. When we are swept up in our emotional story-
lines, we are less likely to take account of the complexity of
the whole situation. It is for this reason that we often regret
what we may say or do when under the influence of emotional
upheaval.

Since the core of emotions is pure aliveness, however, they
are not necessarily problematic. The problematic aspect of
emotional upheaval — its powerful grip and blinding en-
tanglement — is caused by highly-charged dramatic thoughts
and fantasies combining with felt energy. Although thinking
and emotion are usually considered separate mental functions, a close investigation of experience reveals that thinking
plays a key role in generating and maintaining emotional
upheaval. Without the kindling of thoughts and fantasies to
feed on, emotion would be like fire that would quickly burn
out.

The emotional churning of story-lines either is self-destruc-
tive or pollutes the world. It may smolder away inside us,
causing a wide variety of neurotic symptoms, from ulcers to
phobias. Or it may continually "blow off" and spew forth into
the world. It also exaggerates the implications and importance

of our feelings. When we are overcome with depression, which may stem from one specific incident, we tend to see the whole world, our whole life history and future prospects in this light. Our depressed thoughts radiate out in all directions and further intensify the depression. The dramatic story-lines we spin around our emotions lock us into them, keeping them relatively stuck and solidified.

Thus emotional upheavals can be a way of freezing our aliveness, which is quite fluid and open in its basic nature. However, emotions need not become frozen. If we do not try to solidify emotions by churning out elaborate story-lines from them, we may rediscover the intelligence of our basic aliveness in them.

Working with Emotion

What kind of understanding is necessary for the power of emotion to be directly faced in a positive way? How can we relate to emotion without getting stuck in patterns of suppressing it, churning it over, or blindly spewing it out? How may emotion actually become a vehicle for deeper self-knowledge and insight into life?

An important key to working with emotions constructively is facing and examining them without denying them or using them as a weapon for self-justification. Once we decide to work with emotions directly as a vehicle of self-inquiry, there are two different possible approaches: 1) The psychotherapeutic approach, which unfolds the underlying felt meanings contained in emotions. This method, whose steps have been pinpointed in the "Focusing" process developed by Eugene Gendlin, leads to greater personal self-understanding, growth, and effective communication; and 2) The meditative approach, which penetrates through emotions and felt meaning to the ground of basic aliveness from which they arise. Meditation is a more radical practice that can lead to a deeper self-transformation, through the *transmutation* of emotional confusion into great clarity of mind.

The Therapeutic Method

Freeing ourselves from emotional churning through dynamic reflection requires going beneath specific emotions to the broader felt meanings of the situation, as psychotherapist Eugene Gendlin indicates:

> Now, in the situation that is beginning to make me angry, how do I find that move which, if it succeeds, will let me not need to be angry, and which, to succeed, must meet a large number of considerations that make up the situation? I do it from the felt meaning . . . . In contrast, if you focus on the anger, you will get stomping, hitting, kicking, and fighting. The felt meaning implies a vast number of behaviors and verbalizations, and . . . it may imply one suited to all this. The emotion of anger implies fighting. . . If you focus on it, you will get madder and madder[8]

This may sound as though Gendlin is suggesting denying the anger. But actually he is talking about going *through* the anger, letting the anger lead in to the wider context of felt meaning of which anger is only one piece. Going through the emotion to the felt meaning underneath often eases emotional churning and leads to new self-insight.

One client describes it in terms of a hurricane: "If you only go so far into something, it's like going into a hurricane and getting terribly blown about. You have to go into it and keep going further and further *in* till you can see where you are." This beautifully expresses the fact that the direction of focusing is definitely into the emotions, not away from them, yet also that focusing involves something of the centrality, depth, and quiet [of] "being in touch with myself." The felt referent for the moment is *me*. It *unfolds* and is a thousand things. In comparison, the emotional tone which attaches to it and precedes it is not itself a thousand things. To remain with it merely

> feeds it. There is always a "breath-held," tense, tight quality about most of these emotional tones. Yet to turn away from the emotion is to turn away also from the direction in which one "finds oneself." Thus one must "move into" and "through" or "on by" these emotional tones to . . . the *felt meaning* of it all.[9]

Simply venting emotions often causes one to miss seeing important elements in a situation, as in the following example. A woman suddenly tells a man who has been interested in her for a long time that she intends to marry someone else, while also letting him know that he did not pursue her hard enough. The man, who has felt very strongly for her, feels crushed. He could react by getting carried away with anger, self-pity, or resentment. But the situation is actually larger and more meaningful to him than any of these emotional responses would express. Crying or flailing out in this instance do not help him, for, as it turns out, this situation symbolizes or crystallizes a whole pattern of his life. He does feel angry and hurt, but if he can keep going past these emotional tones to get in touch with all of the intensely felt meaning this situation has for him, it can be a powerful opportunity to see deeply into a whole aspect of himself. The loss of this woman he cared about may lead to a realization of how he always plays things safe, not daring to risk himself. He could just cry and forget about it, or instead he could look into the complexity of his feelings that have been aroused by this situation. Perhaps it takes him days to begin really to unravel this complex of felt meaning. But when he finally sees all that is involved in it, he may feel a powerful sense of release, not only from his pain, but also from the blindness of this pattern of behavior he has been trapped in for years. By going into his pain and anger, and seeing what was involved in them, he wakes up to an aspect of his life he has never seen so clearly before. This realization leaves him feeling more in touch with his own life.

Moving through an emotion to open up and reveal the felt meanings underneath is like peeling an onion, layer by layer. As we unfold these meanings, we may gradually feel a release from the emotion's grip. By untangling the knots in emotions and feelings, we arrive momentarily back at the basic ground of our aliveness, which is a moment of both release and freshness. (Gendlin has called this moment a "felt shift.") We also may discover new aspects of ourselves that were previously blocked or screened by habitual emotional story-lines. Then it is more possible to see our way clear to move in directions that are more viable for us, more suited to our whole life situation. Moving through emotional turbulence to untangle its underlying felt meaning and make contact with one's basic aliveness is the core of the psychotherapeutic approach to emotions.

But the limitation of this approach is its tendency to continue exploring further feelings and emotions *rather than to appreciate fully and rest in the basic aliveness that is discovered in moments of shift and opening.* This may result in a continual preoccupation with examining feelings, which can become an endless project, distracting a person from the more basic aliveness, tenderness, and openness he may discover through them.

The Meditative Approach

In meditation, particularly of the mindfulness type, there is no attempt to unravel emotions. Instead, the meditator acknowledges emotions as they are, which eventually allows him to connect directly with a larger dimension of emotional energy.

Feelings and emotions which arise during meditation practice are not seen as having any special importance, as they are in psychotherapy. They are respected as the forms of energy they are, without being "a big deal." While practicing, the meditator does not try to unfold the meanings of his feelings. Rather, he acknowledges the feelings and returns to the discipline of his practice. Feelings and emotions are not an important focus in meditation because the practice is oriented more toward a person's ongoing sense of aliveness than toward the colorations of his passing concerns. Thus meditation cools the heat of emotional fire. If you look at Figure 1 as a wave, then emotional churning is the whitecap where the winds of the world have whipped the ocean into a frenzy. Felt meaning is more like a series of swells, which keep rolling on without any particular climax, while in the depths of the ocean, at the level of basic aliveness, all is quite calm.

In everyday life situations, outside the formal meditation practice, an experienced meditator might also spend less time being wrapped up in the story-lines of his emotions. Whereas we often tend to feel most alive when involved in emotional dramas, meditation practice allows a person to realize how his aliveness is always present, even in undramatic moments, how it is an immediate connection with the world that is much more basic than his particular dramas of the moment. By seeing how he locks himself into particular emotional reactions, he loosens his attachment to them. His emotions are less likely to freeze, and more quickly thaw out to dissolve back into the basic fluidity of his aliveness. He is thus likely to lose his connectedness with the world or to disrupt his life through preoccupation with the self-importance of his feelings. In this way he remains grounded.

Transmutation

This does not mean, however, that someone practicing mindfulness meditation would ignore or suppress his emotions. On the contrary, to the extent that he is not caught up in figuring out all the meanings of his feelings, he could let himself experience the energy and aliveness of his feelings more nakedly, quite apart from the story-lines they suggest. This more radical approach to emotions, which uses them for self-illumination, for seeing through oneself and one's mental fixations, is called *transmutation* in Vajrayana Buddhism as well as in certain other traditions. The notion of transmutation, going back to the ancient alchemical traditions, implies converting something seemingly worthless into something extremely valuable, like lead into gold.

Feeling as Judgment

Seeing through feelings and emotions requires that we understand how they are a judgment of situations in terms of pro or con, pleasant or unpleasant, affirming or negating, acceptance or rejection. Insofar as we continually engage in a project of trying to validate our existence and worth as unique individuals, to achieve a special image of who we are and what we are doing, we feel good when this image is furthered and badly when it is negated or thwarted. Inasmuch as feelings contain these implicit judgments about whether situations affirm or negate us, they take on a positive or negative charge. This preoccupation with affirmation and negation tends to blind us to what is *actually* going on in the situation, beyond how it furthers or defeats our project of becoming somebody important.

We also make more deliberate judgments about feelings and emotions themselves when they arise. For instance, we judge depression negatively, as a "strike against us," while seeing joy or pleasure as affirming us. Being depressed about being depressed puts us at two removes from reality. The struggle against feeling and emotion keeps us locked into emotional churning and may even intensify it.

Befriending Emotions

The first step toward transmutation is to cut through this struggle of self-judgment by accepting emotions as they are. Instead of seeing emotions as a threat, it is possible to befriend them, relate to them as expressions of our own energy. By not indulging in further judgments, we can begin to feel the texture and actual quality of emotions. For someone accustomed to struggling against emotions, this might seem an impossible task — "If I let myself really experience this anger, maybe I will go beserk!" "If I open to this sadness, maybe it will suck me down and sweep me away." In most situations this fear of emotion expresses our alienation from ourselves. By alienating our own energy, making it "other," and then judging it negatively, we come to believe that emotions are demonic, that we may have "monsters" inside us. But fear of fear or anger is much worse than these primary feelings themselves, for it freezes them into a negative form. Running away from a fierce animal, or attempting to suppress it, only provokes attack. The first step in taming the lion of the emotions, in transmuting their seemingly fierce energy into insight and illumination, is to befriend them by allowing them to be, without judging them as good or bad.

Moreover, feelings and emotions are not nearly as substantial as our reactions to them. This lack of solidity and stability is due to the fluid aliveness at their core. Since feelings are continually changing, in-process, they cannot be contemplated or grasped in the same way as the story-lines arising from them. So, if I give up trying to judge my feeling or spin out story-lines from it, if I really open to it, something new may happen.

For example, suppose a man has a misunderstanding with his wife and has to leave for an appointment before it is resolved. As he drives away, he feels a wave of sadness wash over him. His first (automatic) reaction is irritation that he is feeling this sadness, for he does not enjoy the feeling. So he starts by fighting it off. "There must be something wrong with me, maybe I am just a depressed person, here I am feeling this way again." Or: "It's my wife's fault for making me feel this way." These story-lines arise because he is trying to resist feeling the sadness itself.

But suppose instead he lets himself feel genuinely sad, without fighting it or indulging in thoughts about it. No need for all that extra mental churning — what a relief! When he no longer resists it, the sadness is not so claustrophobic. It turns out to have space in it, and he cannot remain stuck in it for very long. He may experience its painfulness more fully, but even this pain reminds him how he is a living being who feels the world inside himself. Letting himself feel this pain, he simultaneously feels his tenderness, his vulnerability to life, his basic aliveness. He feels the naked quality of his life beyond his thoughts, fears, and images. This is a breakthrough which leads to a felt shift. As he opens to it and lets it be, the emotional intensity eases. In turning to face his own demons, they dissolve into his own living energy, which puts him in touch with himself in a whole, fresh way.

Holding on to our emotions is not actually possible, for by their very nature they are ever moving forward. What we hold on to are images, attitudes, or story-lines connected with them, which are not present-oriented, but fixated on past or future events. Emotions may seem to have us in their grip, but as soon as we turn to face them directly, we find nothing so solid as our judgments and avoidances of them.

Emotion as Energy

Thus in facing our emotions, we get a vivid glimpse of the intensity of our existence-as-felt. Emotion, as something we fear or separate ourselves from, may become somewhat stuck. But as something we embody, it is simply a pure process of organismic felt energy, an expression of the dynamic quality of life and its supra-personal nature. As the Tibetan teacher Tarthang Tulku points out:

> The more you go into the disturbance — when you really get in there — the emotional characteristics no longer exist. Then this becomes proper meditation.[10]

The French psychoanalyst Hubert Benoit describes this process of "seeing through" the turbulence of emotion as a "liberating inner gesture," "a looking into one's own nature."[11] This penetration of emotion allows us to feel its dynamic qualities without getting caught in emotionally-charged fantasies. As a gesture of opening directly to the energy of the emotion without backing off, it is simple and direct. There are no tricks involved. As Tarthang Tulku describes it:

> What we can do is concentrate on the anger, not allowing any other thoughts to enter. That means we sit with our angry thoughts, focusing our concentration on the anger — not on its object — so that we make no discriminations, have no reactions. Likewise, when anxiety or any other disturbing feeling arises . . . concentrate on the feeling, not on thoughts about it. Concentrate on the center of the feeling; penetrate into that space. There is a density of energy in that center that is clear and distinct. This energy has great power, and can transmit great clarity . . .
> To transform our negativities, we need only learn to touch them skillfully and gently.[12]

This may be a delicate maneuver at first. We may have a brief glimpse of this larger organismic energy, but then soon drift back into mulling and churning our thoughts, or being seduced by fantasies.

Inner Transformation

The sustained attention that is necessary for this inner work is greatly facilitated by meditation practice, through which a person can learn to stop being "hijacked" by his thoughts. Benoit provides an example of the transmutation that may occur:

> Let us suppose that a failure puts me into a spasm of humiliation; if I take no correct inner action, my humiliation will pass more or less rapidly and sooner or later I will come out of this state; I shall no longer be humiliated, but then I shall have come back to my habitual pretension, and, in consequence, open to an eventual new humiliation. If, on the contrary, in my state of humiliation, I consciously adhere to my spasm, my humiliation disappears without my pretension reappearing . . . my humiliation is transformed into humility.[13]

Various metaphors have been used to describe this transformation of emotional energy. Benoit points out how:

> When a success exalts me, I feel myself to be aggrandized, increased, tenfold in volume; physically even, I feel my chest fill out, my nostrils open, I use large gestures. When, on the contrary, a repulse humiliates me, I feel myself small, shrivelled, reduced. I have a weight on my chest, my gestures are curtailed. The inner action of which we are speaking consists of shutting ourselves up willingly in this reduced volume. There is then produced a sort of condensation of the ego; the ego is at once denied in its volume and affirmed in its density. This process is comparable with that which transforms coal into diamonds; the aim of this process is not the destruction of the ego but its transformation . . . . The conscious acceptance results in the coal which has become denser, and so blacker and more opaque, being instantaneously transformed into a diamond that is perfectly transparent.[14]

Thus emotion may become a window onto the vitality of the life process, itself, transparent to the life force from which it springs. This image of transparency and lucency, like the diamonds metamorphosed from coal, is particularly prominent in Vajrayana (Tantric) Buddhism. *Vajra* signifies the diamond-like, indestructible clarity of the awake state of mind. *Vajra* is itself a quality of life, whose fullest realization is "mirror-like wisdom." Because it signifies absolute clarity, the Vajrayana (literally "diamond path") sees the world in terms of luminosity, lit up with brilliance. Preoccupation with struggling for affirmation against negation screens and distances us from this natural brilliance. Transmutation of emotion is one way of turning the dark, murky world of this mind in struggle into the radiance of clear vision.

This metaphor may make transmutation seem like a sudden change, but it is actually part of a gradual path of increasing friendliness toward oneself. Other metaphors emphasize the organic nature of this process. In Chogyam Trungpa's word:

> Unskilled farmers throw away their rubbish and buy manure from other farmers, but those who are skilled go on collecting their rubbish, in spite of the bad smell and the unclean work, and when it is ready to be used they spread it on the land, and out of this they grow their crops. That is the skilled way . . . . And though it is very difficult and unhygienic, as it were, to work on, that is the only way to start. So out of these unclean things comes the birth of the seed which is Realization.[15]

Suzuki Roshi speaks of how the weeds of the mind may be used to enrich one's awakening awareness:

> We pull the weeds and bury them near the plant to give it nourishment . . . . So you should not be bothered by your mind. You should rather be grateful for the weeds, because eventually they will enrich your practice. If you have some experience of how the weeds in your mind change into mental nourishment, your practice will make remarkable progress.[16]

Thus the intensity of emotion, if allowed to burn itself through, to consume itself without generating further pollution, may actually hasten the disintegration of habitual story-line fixations and fertilize the seed of a larger awareness.

Transmutation in the Buddhist tradition becomes possible only through meditation practice, in which a person learns to face and accept everything that arises in the mind. The meditative way is to befriend emotional energy by discovering in it the intense tenderness of our aliveness.

Identifying with the bodily-felt energy of emotions, instead of emotional dramas, allows us to discover the space and aliveness at their core. Then emotional turmoil appears as a little drama surrounded by a much larger awareness. When we identify with this larger awareness, with the depths of the ocean, rather than with the peaking of the waves, emotions inspire us to commit ourselves more fully to our lives, apart from our struggle to "be somebody." By contrast, treating emotions as intruders grants them dominion over us. "That which has become an object to me is . . . something that has captured me."[17]

Without the proper understanding and guidance, however, opening to intense emotional energy could overrun or inflate a person. Thus it is considered essential in Buddhism to have a firm foundation in meditation practice, which helps a person overcome his domination by thought and fantasy, and become grounded in his own sense of what it means to be alive. It is also considered important to work with a living teacher who has an intimate personal understanding of the energies of life, and who can guide the student through the many twists and turns involved in the development of this larger awareness.

Overcoming fear of our own energy may ultimately lead to a fearlessness toward the whole of life, insofar as there is no longer anything "other" to threaten us. In Buddhism this is known as the "lion's roar."

> The Lion's Roar is the fearless proclamation that any state of mind, including the emotions, is a workable situation. . . . Indian Ashokan art depicts the lion's roar with four lions looking in four directions, which symbolizes the idea of having no back. Every direction is a front, symbolizing all-pervading awareness. The fearlessness covers all directions . . . . Then the most powerful energies become absolutely workable rather than taking you over, because there is nothing to take over if you are not putting up any resistance.[18]

References

1. J. Hillman, *Emotion* (Evanston: Northwestern Univ. Press, 1961), p. 289.

2. S. Freud, *New Introductory Lectures on Psychoanalysis.* (London: Hogarth, 1933). For a further exploration of this aspect of Freud's thought, *see* J. Welwood & K. Wilber, "On Ego Strength and Egolessness," in J. Welwood (Ed.) *The Meeting of the Ways: Explorations in East/West Psychology* (New York: Schocken, 1979).

3. C. G. Jung, *The Integration of the Personality* (London: Routledge & Kegan Paul, 1940), p. 19.

4. J. Hillman, *Re-Visioning Psychology.* (New York: Harper & Row, 1975), p. 175.

5. In J. Needleman (Ed.) *Speaking of My Life: The Art of Living in the Cultural Revolution.* (San Francisco: Harper & Row, 1979), p. 59.

6. E. T. Gendlin, "A Theory of Personality Change." In P. Worchel & D. Byrne (Eds.), *Personality Change.* (New York: Wiley, 1964). E. T. Gendlin et al., "Focusing Ability in Psychotherapy, Personality, and Creativity." In J. Schlien (Ed.), *Research in Psychotherapy,* Vol. III. Washington: American Psychological Association, 1968).
J. Welwood, "Focusing, Self-Actualization, and Therapy Behavior," Unpublished Master's Dissertation, University of Chicago, 1969.

7. E. T. Gendlin, *Focusing.* (New York: Everest House, 1979).

8. E. T. Gendlin, "A Phenomenology of Emotions: Anger." In D. Carr & E. Casey (Eds.), *Explorations in Phenomenology.* (The Hague: Martinus Nijhoff, 1973), p. 394.

9. E. T. Gendlin, "A Theory of Personality Change," p. 124n.

10. Tarthang Tulku, "On Thoughts." *Crystal Mirror,* 1974, 3, p. 18.

11. H. Benoit, *The Supreme Doctrine.* (New York: Viking, 1959), p 130.

12. Tarthang Tulku, *Openness Mind.* (Emeryville, CA.: Dharma, 1978), pp. 52, 54.

13. H. Benoit, op cit., p. 143.

14. *Ibid.,* p. 143.

15. C. Trungpa, *Meditation in Action.* (Boulder: Shambhala, 1969), p. 23.

16. S. Suzuki, *Zen Mind, Beginner's Mind.* (New York: Walker, Weatherhill, 1970), p. 36.

17. S. Hisamatsu, "The Characteristics of Oriental Nothingness." In R. DeMartino (Transl.), *Philosophical Studies of Japan,* Vol. 2, (Tokyo: Maruzen, 1960), p. 78.

18. C. Trungpa, *The Myth of Freedom*. (Boulder: Shambhala, 1976), pp. 69-72.

John Welwood, Ph.D., has a private counseling practice in San Francisco, and is Associate Professor at the California Institute of Asian Studies. He is an editor of and frequent contributor to both the *Journal of Transpersonal Psychology* and *Re-Vision*. He has recently published *The Meeting of the Ways: Explorations in East/West Psychology* (New York: Schocken, 1979).

$>7<$

ORGANISMIC PROCESS: A PARADIGM FOR FREEING HUMAN CREATIVITY
Martha Crampton

INTRODUCTION

Humankind is at a crossroads. We seem to have reached a juncture in our evolutionary process where the directions we choose can produce a quantum jump in evolutionary momentum. There is the possibility of expressing new levels of creative order and wholeness. There is the alternative of fragmentation and chaos or the totalitarian order of Orwell's *1984*. The choices we make will reflect the world views we hold.

This period is marked by an unprecedented acceleration of change. Experts of many varieties avow their incapability to predict the future. None of the theories or methods we have relied on in the past seems adequate to deal with today's world — whether this be the world of economics or politics, physics or psychology. There is a widespread sense of the need for a new paradigm.

I believe that the essence of the needed paradigm shift is from a mechanistic to an organismic world view. We must learn to perceive ourselves and the universe as animate, intentional, organic wholes in self-creating process rather than as inanimate things.

The metaphysical basis for this shift, process-organismic metaphysics, has been a minority position in Western philosophy since Aristotle. In recent decades, process metaphysics has reached a high stage of development, particularly in the works of such philosophers as Whitehead and Hartshorne.

The logical basis for this paradigm shift is also being developed. This century has seen crises in the foundations of mathematics spur research into the foundations of logic. It is clear that what we now know as conventional bi-polar logic is but one tiny and primitive fragment of an infinite variety of logics. We need to develop new logical foundations for an organismic paradigm to come to grips with dimensions of life where conventional logic breaks down — areas such as values, intentionality, and paradox.

With these foundations in mind, and with my experience in working with processes of creative synthesis in indivduals and groups as a practitioner of psychosynthesis, I have formed some hypotheses about organizing principles in the animate universe. I am working toward the development of a science of living processes or organismic wholes which I have chosen to call "holodynamics,"* to emphasize its foundations in holism and dynamic process. My conviction is that such a science, though yet in its infancy, offers the hope of a ground on which to stand in responding to the challenges of our turbulent times.

---

*I wish to acknowledge the contribution to this work of my partner, Norman Hirst, whose years of exploring the foundations of physics, mathematics, formal logic, general systems, and value theory have helped to make possible this next step in our own creative process. His assistance in the preparation of this paper has been invaluable.

In the following section, I will set forth some basic postulates of organismic process or "holodynamics." I will then discuss the need for an organismqc world view. The major part of the paper will present principles and techniques of human development derived from my practice of psychosynthesis, as they relate to the postulates of holodynamics. In the concluding section, I will develop some thoughts about implications of these principles for the design of social structures to enhance human creativity.

POSTULATES

1. The universe is an evolutionary process or organismic whole aiming toward higher orders of creative synthesis. It has the properties of a living being rather than those of an inanimate mechanism.

2. Creative synthesis is a process whereby contrasting elements are harmonized and integrated to form more complex organismic wholes. The goal and result of this process is increased value.

3. This process implies a hierarchical order in which the "higher" order or level of organization provides formal or structural principles which act as delimiting constraints for the integration of lower-order entities within itself. In other words, the higher order acts as contentless form ("forma") which shapes the raw material ("materia") of the lower order (allowing for freedom of choice of the lower-order entities).

4. An entity, system, or process may or may not be organismic.

5. An organismic entity is characterized by self-organization.

6. The self-organizing process of an organismic entity is carried out by a center of consciousness and will that we shall call its "Creative Center" or "regnant nexus" (Whitehead's term). Note: the consciousness and will of entities at different levels of the "chain of Being" would reflect their different stages of evolutionary development.

7. The concept of self-organization includes the following:
   — a center or nexus of consciousness and will that directs the process of self-organization;
   — self-responsibility and free will of this organizing center;

— increasing integration of the organism's component parts, according to the principles of creative synthesis;
— integrity of the organism's boundaries;
— a cybernetic process whereby the Creative Center adjusts its input signals according to feedback from the component parts of the organism and input from a supraordinate Creative Center.

8. In its process of evolution through creative synthesis, the universe seems to be "learning" in a particular way. This kind of learning may be called organismic or holistic, as it involves the whole entity — will and heart as well as mind.

9. This kind of organismic learning is the "name of the game," the purpose of the process, at all levels of the hierarchy. It increases the organism's level of organization and bears the fruits of wisdom rather than mere knowledge.

10. The content of this learning seems to be the principles and methods of the creative evolutionary process itself — i.e., learning to exercise free will in self-creation, with increasing degrees of love and intelligence. (Note: "Love" in this context is a principle of aggregation that implies intrinsic valuation. Intelligence is viewed as a principle of effectiveness for a given purpose. It implies an understanding of organizing principles, as choice of the optimal path requires using these principles. The law of economy or "doing more with less" is an example of intelligence in operation.

11. The process of creative synthesis is carried out through two complementary principles: differentiation and integration. Differentiation produces multiplicity. Integration combines differentiated entities into more complex wholes.

12. In the case of organismic entities, the complementary processes of differentiation and integration must be in dynamic equilibrium.

13. Every living entity is simultaneously a "whole" within itself and a "part" within a larger matrix.

14. An organismic entity (such as a human being) cannot be integrated into a more complex organismic entity (such as the planet or certain social structures) until it has reached a

critical point in its process of differentiation or individualization. The principle is that the lower-order entity must maintain its individual identity when it is integrated into the higher-order entity.

15. If such integration is attempted prematurely, the aliveness and creativity of both the lower-order and the higher-order entity will be diminished.

16. When higher-order integration is attempted before the lower-order organism has achieved a requisite degree of individualization, the lower-order entity may respond in two basic ways: primitive fusion or encapsulization (often with some oscillation between them). In the case of primitive fusion, the lower-order entity loses its boundaries and abdicates its self-organizing principle to the higher order. In the case of encapsulization, the lower-order entity augments its boundaries to preserve its identity. In both cases, the entity's individualization process is distorted and delayed.

17. As human beings we can discover the principles and techniques of evolutionary process or self-creation, and apply them in our own lives. As we increase our ability to consciously cooperate with evolutionary process, our experience of life purpose, meaning, and value is enhanced.

The Need for an Organismic View

The need to believe that the universe is unfolding according to a lawful process seems to be a fundamental need of human beings. Without this we feel lost, despairing, and deprived of something essential to the experience of value and meaning in our lives. This fact was brought home to me in a dramatic way in a workshop I led. I gave instructions to the group to "try on" a world view in which the universe was seen as arbitrary, as lacking order and purpose. They were told to imagine what it would be like to live in such a world and to observe the effects of this world view on their thoughts, feelings, and behavior. The reactions in the group ranged from apathy and depression to rage and a search for titillation. The latter even took the form, in one sub-group, of deliberate plotting to murder and pillage — just for the thrill of it. Their violence seemed to express a profound sense of anger and frustration at the loss of life meaning, a desire to drown out the pain of this, and an indifference to life in a world without human value. As one person put it, "If there is no order in the universe, then nothing matters. So why not kill?"

I believe that the path, which we as a species will choose at the crossroads facing us today, will be decided largely by our understanding of the cosmic order — in particular whether we view it as a living, organismic order or the lifeless order of a mechanical system.

DYNAMICS OF ORGANISMIC PROCESS
APPLIED TO HUMAN DEVELOPMENT

In the following part of this paper, I will discuss some practical issues of human development as they relate to the dynamics of organismic process or "holodynamics." I will focus on areas which I have found to be of particular importance in working with people in psychosynthesis. The principles involved in differentiation of the personality as an integrated entity will be the primary focus, and will be used as the basis for extrapolation to higher orders of organismic process.

Complementarity of Differentiation and Integration — the "Janus Effect"

As our postulates state, every organismic entity is simultaneously a "whole" and a "part." Expression of both aspects is necessary to the organism's fulfillment. This complementarity has been called the "Janus effect" by Arthur Koestler, after the Roman god who had two faces looking in opposite directions. When entities are viewed as wholes, they are like the face that looks "downward" in a hierarchical system — i.e., they are self-assertive entities which organize their constituent parts and have autonomy in their own domain. When viewed as parts, they are like the face that looks "upward" in a hierarchy — i.e., they in turn become sub-wholes within a greater whole. Koestler has coined the term "holon" to refer to the Janus-faced entities which comprise a hierarchic order. He sees such hierarchies as "a universal characteristic of life."

As the Janus effect applies to human development, we need to view the human organism as a hierarchy of holons which exert their "regnant nexus" at different stages in the developmental process. The holon with which we will be primarily concerned with in this paper is that of the integrated personality, which is governed by a Creative Center called the "I" in psychosynthesis. The personality itself is constituted of three primary holons: a physical body, an emotional "body," and a concrete mental "body." These sub-systems of the personality (sometimes called "vehicles" or "sheaths" in Eastern philosophy) have various levels of organization within themselves. Thus the physical body is constituted of systems, organs, tissues, cells, molecules, atoms, sub-atomic particles, etc. Through the aeons of evolution which it shares with the animal kingdom, the physical holon has achieved a marvelous degree of creative synthesis. Were it not for the disorder in our emotional and mental vehicles, the physical body would function smoothly. A major evolutionary task now facing us is to integrate our emotional and mental "bodies" so that they too can function as harmonious wholes. This means that we will need to learn much more about the sub-systems within these bodies and about the methods for their integration. The "I" as the Creative Center of the personality has the task of developing, coordinating, and harmonizing the three personality vehicles to form an integrated personality which eventually becomes an organismic holon in its own right.

Learning the Principles of Self-Organization

To accomplish its task as Creative Center of the personality holon, the "I," like any "regnant nexus," must learn the principles and skills of self-organization. This involves several things. The "I" must first of all become conscious of itself as a source of creative will and take responsibility for the governance of its own domain. It must preserve the integrity of the organism's boundaries, and learn to integrate the component parts of the personality according to principles of value (creative synthesis through free will expressed with love and intelligence). It must also discover the methods by which it can direct the personality vehicles in the fulfillment of its purpose.

Under present cultural conditions, the task of learning which faces the "I" is long and arduous. Many people go through their whole lives without being able to integrate their personality. Making the principles and skills of self-organization more widely known would be a great contribution to human creativity and happiness, and to our ability to live in peace with one another.

Self-Responsibility and Relating to Error

An important aspect of self-organization is the learning of self-responsibility. One of the greatest barriers to this process is the misconception we have about what responsibility means. Most people react to the word as though it meant an onerous burden. The deeper cause of this seems to lie in our misunderstanding of error. We are conditioned from childhood to believe that being wrong means being "bad," and we are afraid of being responsible because we don't want to be wrong. In our dread of making mistakes, we cover them up when they do occur. Thus we miss a valuable opportunity to learn from experience. Our needless anxiety also makes us clumsy and narrow in our approach. All of this adds up to a heavy brake on the creative process. The time has come to take error out of the closet and to give it a place of honor as one of our greatest teachers. I can truly say that, among the gurus in my own life, the ones with the most transformative effect have been the tailor-made lessons of my own mistakes.

The "I," quite understandably, tends to get caught at first in the prevailing beliefs about error. When it is governed by the fear of being wrong, it loses its true identity as a source of creative will. It becomes identified with the popular games designed to avoid the experience of error: blaming, passing the buck, playing victim, etc. When people are trapped in these "false identities," they lose touch with their Creative Center. A little training in the art of making mistakes may be very helpful at this point. Such people need to be reminded that error is an inevitable part of being human, that the only real mistake is the failure to learn from our mistakes — and even this must be forgiven.

Transmutation of Error to Learning

The key to transmuting error creatively, at least when it has involved significant harm to oneself or others, is to find the right vantage point from which to view it. This implies an open heart — being able to perceive the error with clarity and compassion and to be touched at a depth level by this perception. It requires that the person see accurately the blind spots and unskillful behavior which created the situation, and that the pain of damage caused be adequately experienced. When this occurs, there is frequently an experience of compassionate sorrow — a cleansing process which theology calls "contrition" — that the person must go through as part of his or her healing. When the natural cycle is completed, it brings a realignment of the will — a "turning around" (the root meaning of "conversion") of one's orientation. The will is released to move forward in a new direction and the past is forgiven.

It is of vital importance to distinguish between the redemptive experience of contrition and a neurotic attitude of self-condemnation — a distinction which is little understood in the therapeutic field. Paradoxical as it may seem, feeling "guilty" actually prevents us from perceiving error in a transformative way. It blocks us from seeing clearly because we are more concerned with self-flagellation than we are with understanding what happened. The defensiveness engendered by feeling guilty also closes the heart and does not allow us to be truly touched by the meaning of the experience. It is an interestng fact that the heart is traditionally associated both with vision and with spiritual will. The ageless wisdom tells us that we can see clearly only with the "eye of the heart," that love alone can reveal truth. We must set aside the distorting lens of compassionless judgment so that the eye of the heart may be opened and we may know the grace of transformation.

Maintaining Organismic Boundaries

Another skill involved in self-organization is learning to maintain the integrity of the organism's boundaries. This the "I" does largely through self-responsibility. When we fail to

take responsibility for the fact that we create our own feelings, we may believe that other people have the power to
"make us angry." In the act of blaming others, we lose our
own ego boundaries and we become disconnected from our
own causal principle.

An important concept in maintaining the integrity of our
organismic boundaries is what I call the "auric field." The
auric field is the domain — the sacred ground — for which we
have primary responsibility in this lifetime. It is comprised of
the interpenetrating energy fields (physical, emotional, mental, and beyond) which constitute our subtle structure. This
subtle aspect of our constitution has long been recognized by
spiritual tradition and is now being documented by
technologies such as Kirlian photography. Clairvoyants who
perceive these energy fields refer to them collectively as the
"aura" and sometimes speak of the "auric egg" because of its
ovoid form.

To protect the auric field, the "I" must own its power and
responsibility as the Creative Center of the personality. It must
also learn some skills for avoiding situations which could
violate the aura.

"Disidentification" of the "I" from Environing Forces

The initial step in self-responsibility is for the "I" to dif-
ferentiate itself from the various forces around it. These include both the urges of the personality (the inner environment) and the pressures of the external environment. It must
learn that its own nature is of a different order from that of its
"surroundings," that it need not passively react to the pushes
and pulls around it. This "disidentification" process goes
through several stages. At first the "I" discovers a still place in
consciousness like the eye within a hurricane, where it can
observe the phenomena of its experience without being con-
trolled by them. Having attained this "observer" position, we
can observe an emotion such as fear within ourselves without
having to act on the basis of this fear.

The next step is for the "I" to learn that it is an active,
causal principle within its own domain. In other words, it must
realize itself as a source of intentionality, of initiatory and
creative will. From being reactive, it becomes proactive. It

begins to explore various ways of shaping and directing the forces around it. Through feedback from the environment, it discovers the effects of different ways of expressing its intentionality. In this process it gradually transmutes the clumsiness of "strong will" into a more sensitive and adaptive approach, and learns to include the principles of love and intelligence. This aspect has been discussed by Assagioli in his book, *The Act of Will,* which presents some psychological laws for "doing more with less."

Taking Responsibility for our Auric Field

In order to exercise self-responsibility within the auric field, the "I" must acquire certain basic insights. These include:
— the "I" as Creative Center of the personality has dominion over its own auric field — i.e., it has the power to choose whether to include, to exclude, or to transmute the thoughts or feelings that come within its domain;
— the choice to energize particular classes of thoughts or feelings has definite consequences in both our internal and external worlds;
— that these consequences may be life-enhancing or life-negating for ourselves, for other organisms, and for the world; and
— that we are ultimately responsible for the thoughts we hold and their effects; and that our choices in this domain determine the course of our evolution.
We must eventually learn that, just as we do not allow a demented stranger to enter our home and destroy our living space, so we must exercise discernment in respect to the thoughts and feelings we entertain.

Thoughts that Interfere with Creative Evolution

Specifically, some major classes of thoughts which block creative evolution are:
— those which assume that the world, including ourselves, is thing-like rather than process-like in character;
— those which violate the principle of unconditional love for oneself or others;
— those which violate freedom of the will — i.e., which

attempt, consciously or unconsciously, to impose our will on other people, either directly through force or indirectly through manipulation.

Thoughts that Assume Thingness

As human beings we implicitly view ourselves as "things" when we identify with our behaviors or the existing attributes of our personality instead of identifying with the spiritual essence which underlies our personality expression. We become thing-like when we identify with concrete forms such as the roles or "games" we play, the things we own, or a particular aspect of our physical, emotional, or mental experience. Because we confuse these "false identifications" with our essence or Creative Center, we are afraid to let go of them. We cling to what is familiar even when it is clearly not working. It is not uncommon to see people so identified with their existing behavioral expression that they sincerely believe that they cannot change. When they get a glimpse of some emerging potential, they will quickly deny it, saying "I could never be that way; it would be totally out of character for me." This notion of "being out of character" reflects the pernicious belief that we are fated to remain the way we have been in the past, that growth and change are wrong, frightening, or simply unthinkable. This pattern is reflected on a larger scale in the well-known rigidity and resistance to change of our social institutions. We must find ways to help people and larger scale entities disidentify from their existing behaviors so that they can become open to creative transformation. To do this they must be helped to recognize their "spiritual" identity as an agent of creative process, as a conscious participant in the on-going mystery of Creation. They must experience themselves as living organisms rather than as inanimate things.

Thoughts which Violate the Principle of Unconditional Love

Love as an evolutionary principle is unconditional. That is to say, it places no conditions or limitations on the giving of itself. It is related to the concept of goodwill and is concerned with supporting the evolution and well-being of the loved one.

The recipient of unconditional love is intrinsically valued — i.e., is valued for what he/she is, in him-/herself, rather than for the sake of some extrinsic end. This principle precludes manipulation of the loved one and necessitates respect for the person's free-will.

We must begin by giving ourselves unconditional love. Without this we cannot truly love another. This means that we must eliminate the perfectionist pattern of loving ourselves only when we have measured up to some unattainable standard of perfection. We must love ourselves exactly as we are now, with all our warts and frailties, knowing that we are exactly where we need to be for our own growth.

An important step in the expression of unconditional love is the realization that we *are* a source of love. It is a dramatic and liberating insight for people to "get" that they do not have to sit around feeling sorry for themselves while they wait for someone else to love them; that they have the power within themselves to *initiate* the expression of infinite unconditional love, and thus to become Love.

We often fear loving another person because we believe it is a sign of weakness or that we may get ripped off in some way. We need to learn that "coming from Love" is the strongest place to come from, and that the power of love to transform a difficult situation is often nothing short of miraculous. When we relate to a person from love, we are supporting their essence or Creative Center, and thus we are more likely to evoke the person's best qualities. In unconditional love there is no fear; instead we are sustained by the spirit of peace within us. If we are to eliminate war in its many manifestations, we must learn that we have the power to choose peace and develop methods to help make this choice a more common one.

Thoughts which Violate Freedom of Will

We can violate the auric field of a person in many ways, including the holding of strong negative thoughts about that person. Such violation is an infringement upon the free will of the person, particularly when it involves a subtle form of manipulation which is not fully conscious to the individuals concerned. The extent to which we manipulate one another through emotional weapons such as guilt, fear, and conditional love is not fully appreciated.

The laws of creative synthesis require that we protect our own auric field and respect that of other persons. We can protect ourselves by taking responsibility for the fact that we create our own subjective states, and by avoiding exposure to situations of violence — whether this violence be physical, emotional, or mental. If we refuse to play a victim role, we do not need to be angry or resentful. Simple communication skills can be taught for doing this without making the other person "bad." The keys lie in acknowledging both our own power and our own vulnerability, and in assuming the other person's goodwill. When one person takes responsibility to observe the laws of "right human relations," this supports the best interests of both parties. We need to realize that we are not doing people a favor by allowing them to manipulate us and, in so doing, to harm themselves.

Integration of the Personality Holon within the Self Holon

When the personality is sufficiently differentiated as an integrated holon in its own right, it can be included as a cooperative part in a higher-order holon. The organizing principle or Creative Center of this more inclusive regnant nexus is called the "Self" in psychosynthesis. It corresponds to the spiritual essence recognized by most religions and known by such names as the "soul," the "atman," or the "higher Self." When the personality is sufficiently integrated to serve as "materia" or as a vehicle of expression for the Self, the higher-order nexus gradually becomes dominant over the more self-centered nexus of the personality. As the person's sense of identitybshifts "upward," the consciousness and sphere of influence is expanded, and the person becomes concerned with service from a more global perspective.

A Higher-Order Creative Center Beyond the Self Concerned with Planetary Purposes

There is reason to believe that yet another organizing center or holon comes into play in the case of more evolved human beings. Certain metaphysical systems speak of such a center as the "monad" or the "universal Self." It may be that we experience this center (or the highest order Creative Center we are able to contact) as God.

It seems reasonable to hypothesize, by extrapolation, that such a center would express itself through vehicles of more refined substance (substance at a higher vibratory level) than that of the personality vehicles, though it would subsume the latter. As a person becomes capable of responding to these subtler energy fields beyond the Self, he/she begins to attune to higher orders of planetary will, love, and intelligence. At this point the person usually experiences a sense of unfolding vocation or "calling" and senses that he/she has a unique and necessary part to play within the planetary purpose — much like being a cell within the planetary body. As a cell the person then joins with other cells in the creation of more complex structures to accomplish their common ends. Such structures (need we add?) must be organismic if they are to carry the "high voltage" of planetary purpose without being shattered.

Though we will not speculate further here on this subject, it seems important to be aware of higher-order Creative Centers as we begin to study the planet as an organism.

The Archetype of the Creative Center: Methods of Study

Though science has not yet demonstrated the tangible existence of a "Creative Center" at any level of organization, much less its mode of operation, there are many clues now available from diverse disciplines which point in the same direction and may eventually produce a breakthrough.

We have indirect evidence bearing on the existence of a Creative Center at various levels from introspective data and from the testimony of religious experience. The depth imagery of the unconscious as found in myth, ritual, religious and alchemical symbolism, dream, art, and guided imagination, provides many useful insights into the archetype of the Creative Center. There are also fascinating clues to be found in the cosmic imagination as we see it reflected in such phenomena as DNA, black holes, resonance effects, the laws of harmony, and the phenomena of electro-magnetism. Work in the new physics such as the research on sub-atomic group structures and David Bohm's ideas about the "enfolded" and "unfolded" universe, may also help us to refine our understanding of the Creative Center.

Some of the most promising data now seems to be coming in through the discipline of General Systems Theory, as well as through certain lesser-known developments in modern formal logic. For example, the class of formalisms known as combinatory logic enables us to study the foundations of logic itself and to handle phenomena such as paradox which have frustrated traditional logic. In addition, the new meta-discipline of logic called epitheory can generate an infinite variety of logics appropriate to the various "perspectives" from which we can usefully view the world. It is my hunch that through the convergence of such disciplines we will find essential insights into organismic process.

Properties of Organismic and Non-Organismic Systems

Both organismic and non-organismic systems are constructed of various hierarchical levels through which communication and control in the system are carried out. The various elements in both types of system interface with one another to contribute their skills to the task of the system.

In a mechanical or non-organismic system the components are ordered in a deterministic fashion and must respond in a preordained way. In an organismic system, each level of the living reality is an evolving, self-organizing process in itself with a built-in principle of free will. Thus constraints or organizing principles imposed upon a lower-order Creative Center from the next level up, act more as an invitation or a "calling" than a machine-like order. In a human being the influence of the higher-order system may be experienced as controlling when the personality is not yet established as an autonomous entity. This illusion is a major source of resistance to the higher Self.

The constraints for a lower-order Creative Center are developed by the higher-order center through a combination of four variables: the universal principles of creative synthesis, which operate at all levels; the logic inherent in the realm of "materia" concerned; the particular formative or organizing principles required to guide the next step in the lower-order entity's development; and the constraints on this development which render it compatible for integration within the higher-order system. These four variables are combined by the higher-order Creative Center to form a "steering program" for the lower-order center which expresses the purpose or intentionality of the higher-order center.

The lower-order Creative Center must be able to identify with the more inclusive purpose of the higher-order Center in order to freely cooperate with it. Thus the purpose of the higher-order Center must be experienced as something to be "embraced" rather than as something imposed. The lower-order organism finds its will "attracted" to the more inclusive purpose through the principles of "love" and "intelligence" as defined in our postulates. In the case of a human being, the love and intelligence aspects (the emotional and mental "bodies") may have developed at the same rate or one may be more highly evolved than the other. In persons of a more emotional nature, embracing the higher-order purpose ("the will of God") may be experienced as a mystical marriage. Hence the term "bridal chamber mysticism" used by certain historians. In the case of persons whose mental development is dominant, the alignment of wills comes about primarily through understanding of the principles involved. In order for a complete union of wills to take place, all the "bodies" of the lower-order entity (the personality) must be "in resonance" with the higher-order field. This implies integration within and among themselves.

In non-organismic systems, the component parts are manufactured in series and are replaceable by another component of the same type. Their behavior is relatively predictable. In organismic systems, each component is unique and irreplaceable. Its behavior is unpredictable. When organismic components have differentiated as self-responsible entities, they discover that they have a unique and necessary part to play within a larger matrix. In order to find fulfillment of their life purpose, human beings need to express their uniqueness.

They need to do what is theirs alone to do. They will either resist violently or suffer spiritual death when treated as cogs in a machine.

In non-organismic systems, the various levels of organization are governed by the logic inherent in the space-time manifold — i.e., the logic of mathematics. There may be a variety of formal structures in the system, within the overall context of this logic. Thus in a computer system, we may have the following levels and formal structures.

Levels	Formal Structures
circuit components	physics
circuits	engineering circuit theory
logic circuits	boolean algebra
programming	effective processes

As we move from the lower level (components) we find increasingly complex elements being coordinated to carry out more complex processes. These elements, however, all conform to the logic of mathematics.

In the living universe we find, by contrast, various dimensions as well as levels of reality. The dimensions are cfaracterized by different logics. Within a dimension there is a continuity of logics, though different levels within the dimension may have different formal structures. Between dimensions there is discontinuity in terms of their logic. There is thus the need for a particular type of interface processor to connect the "logic" of discontinuous realms. Such is the role of the Self in the human organism. It has the function of interfacing our four-dimensional world of space and time with an other-dimensional order in which space and time as we know them are no longer relevant. Thus persons who have had certain kinds of mystical or near-death experiences report a sense of timelessness where everything seems to exist simultaneously.

How an Organismic System Learns

An organismic system is a self-organizing process. This also means that it is a learning process. A self-organizing process is one which, in response to experience, constructs an evolving structure. Increased skills are developed in the process. Thus, the self-organizing system "learns."

In operation, the Creative Center must, like Janus, "look" in two opposite directions. It must be cognizant of the entities within its own domain — i.e., the sub-entities comprising the entity which it (the Creative Center) is organizing. It must also be aware of the requirements it must satisfy as part of a larger whole.

A Creative Center is the principle of intentionality or will within an organismic system. It is learning to express its will according to the laws of creative synthesis within a particular domain. These laws are meta-principles. How they operate at a given level depends on the logic and "materia" of that level. Thus a Creative Center must learn how the laws of creative synthesis operate at the level with which it is concerned and must develop methods for wielding these laws effectively. In the case of the "I," for example, the "materia" of its domain is the physical, emotional, and mental bodies. Learning, for the "I," means discovering the principles and techniques for integrating the personality vehicles into a harmonious and differentiated whole.

Cybernetic Relations Between Self and the "I"

The relationship between the Self and the "I" is similar to the relationship shown in the diagram below for an adaptive cybernetic system.

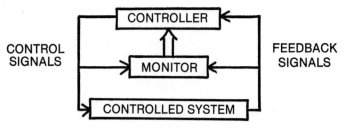

If we left out the monitor we would have a simple cybernetic system. By placing the monitor in the system, the monitor can observe system performance and send information to the controller for changing the performance of the system.

The Self corresponds to the monitor; the "I" to the controller. As a higher-order Creative Center tuned to a different logic, the Self cannot function at the same level as the "I." Nevertheless, the Self is learning and evolving through its experience with the "I."

The "I" learns by doing and by getting feedback on what it does. This feedback is of two kinds. It gets feedback from its interactions with the environment. This may take diverse forms from "a punch in the nose" to successful completion of a project or experiment. The "I" also receives feedback from the Self. This feedback may be inaudible when the "noise" in the system is too great. The feedback from the Self to the "I" is usually experienced as a positive or negative feeling tone. In the practice of Ignatian discernment, this is referred to as "consolation" and "desolation." When the "I" is receiving positive feedback, the experience is generally characterized by a sense of inner peace, joy, or lightness. In the case of negative feedback, there is an experience of guilt, anxiety, oppression, or heaviness. There is a particular quality to this "still small voice of conscience" which differentiates it from imposter voices, such as neurotic guilt or "should's." The feedback of the Self functions to increase awareness of the laws of creative synthesis.

Early in life, the inexperienced "I" faces the problem of survival. Lacking the power to survive on its own, and the child develops skills and techniques which reflect its dependency. If the child succeeds, its success can validate the implicit belief structure, which may then be carried into adult life. The most common dysfunctional patterns of adults are built around beliefs constructed by an immature organism — e.g., that the source of love, power, and wisdom lies outside oneself, and that it is necessary to manipulate other people to get one's needs met. These beliefs must be transformed by feedback from the environment and from the Self.

The "Language" of the Self: Abstract Pattern

The native language of the Self seems to be that of the abstract mind — a transpersonal dimension of our nature which mediates our perception of higher-order context and meaning. This is a language of abstract pattern, structure, and relationship. Unlike the concrete mind, which is concerned with immediate concrete fact, the abstract mind is concerned with organizing principles.

The abstract mind appears to be the mental vehicle of the Creative Center beyond the Self which we shall call the Monad. The intentionality of the Monad is concerned with higher orders of integration within the planetary purpose. Thus the abstract mind is the repository of the true "leading edge" ideas or the emergent paradigms at any point in the cultural evolution of the planet. This realm has been called by such names as the "noosphere" (Teilhard de Chardin), the "planetary field of mind" (Elmer Green), and the "raincloud of knowable things" (Patanjali). It underlies the notion of "an idea whose time has come," and would explain the fact that different people at a given point in history simultaneously discover the same ideas. Thus, Liebnitz and Newton independently developed the calculus.

When the abstract mental vehicle of a person is sufficiently developed, the Self communicates by conveying a sense of pattern or structure which is registered in an immediate "right brain" kind of way. The logic of the structural relationships must then be worked out by a more linear type of processing that we have come to associate with the "left brain." (The question of hemispheric specialization, however, is more complex than this.)

Complete mental development brings the ability to use both the concrete and abstract mental vehicles effectively, as well as the ability to coordinate them. The bridging skill is necessary in order to translate abstract principles into practical action in the world. When a person has not yet developed the abstract mental vehicle, the Self communicates in language which appears to be indirect and metaphorical. It is obliged to use less precise modes of communication because its native language is not accessible to the person. In such cases it uses the language of imagery and feeling tone to communicate emergent patterns. This imagery can be of various kinds, with visual and kinesthetic imagery being the most common. The language of imagery and archetypal symbolism, if studied in a meditative way, can be a useful way to develop our pattern recognition function. It is necessary, however, to seek the abstract or formal structure behind the concrete image, which otherwise can be misleading.

An interesting technique called "experiential focusing" has recently been described by Gendlin, based on the use of kinesthetic imagery. It involves contacting an "organismic awareness" of emergent process through focusing on one's "felt sense" of this. A "felt sense" includes an aspect of physical sensation and an aspect of feeling, though it goes beyond both to a more holistic kind of awareness.

The Self also communicates "symbolically" through the patterns of events in our lives. The phenomena of synchronicity or meaningful coincidence are widely discussed. The "laws of karma," as Eastern philosophy calls them, are now recognized as a pattern behind the pattern by many Occidentals as well. It appears that the laws of karma act in such a way that, when we violate value principles, the universe fills in our blind spot through a balancing process.

Our "Internal Guidance System"

The Self, like other Creative Centers, operates through a cybernetic process. This process provides an "internal guidance system" which functions to optimize the path of the "I's" evolution. When we grasp the significance of this process, we know ourselves to be totally supported by the universe.

Learning to Communicate with the Self: The Role of Education

Most of us receive little help from our cultural institutions in learning to "read out" the information we are receiving from the Self. Although the Self "tries hard," much of its effort is wasted because of our lack of basic literacy in this most important human language. How can education help? Perhaps the basic attitude with which education might concern itself is teaching people to value their internal experience — to find it interesting, to pay attention to it, to take it both seriously and playfully. Educators could help students to establish what Carl Rogers calls an "internal locus of valuation" — taking responsibility for their own choices and their own mistakes. Skills pertaining to exploration of value principles could be taught. These might include techniques such as "experiential focusing," visualization, guided imagination, meditation, and study of areas such as archetypal symbolism and abstract principles in all the fields of knowledge. Application of the principles and techniques of self-creation to one's own life, however, is the most important laboratory for this type of learning.

Organismic Listening: The Method of Invocation and Evocation

Conscious communication with our source of inner guidance requires a particular kind of attitude, an "organismic" kind of listening. This means that as a Creative Center of organismic intention, we are reaching out to a higher-order Center of organismic intention. We can assume that the higher-order Center "desires" to communicate with us, providing we ask the right question and are willing and able to respond wisely. This attitude requires a kind of reaching out with "active receptivity" — a paradoxical state of volition which is simultaneously a thrusting forward and a patient waiting. This attitude, which has been called "invocation," involves a joint activity of will, heart, and mind. The focused intentionality of the invocative attitude evokes a response from the internal guidance system. The techniques of invocation and evocation will no doubt become an important field of study when organismic process is more widely understood.

In order to discern the voice of guidance, we need to quiet the clatter of the many other voices within us. Without this, "noise in the system" may distort the message or render it inaudible. The major sources of "noise" are emotional turbulence, negative attitudes, and attachments to preconceived ways of doing and thinking. It has been well said that if a room is full of clutter, it leaves no room for the Lord to enter. We must "clean house" before we turn toward a higher-order Center. We must be open enough to perceive patterns that are different from those we are accustomed to and which may even obey a different "logic." And we must have enough flexibility to experiment with new ways of being and doing in response to the promptings of the life principle within us. When we learn to stand without attachments and committed to "Thy will be done," it is as though a powerful vortex were created, drawing down inspiration and guidance.

APPLICATIONS OF THE ORGANISMIC PARADIGM TO SOCIAL STRUCTURE

Human Evolution Requires a Change in Social Forms

We have reached a point in human history where, for the first time, it seems possible to create social structures of a new kind. The social structures we have had in the past have reflected the general level of human development at that time. Average humanity, until quite recently, has been at a quite immature stage of organismic development. Most people were caught in survival patterns and primitive forms of defensive behavior. They were far from having attained the status of self-responsible differentiated entities. They lacked the basic knowledge and skills required for personality integration and were not particularly interested in the subject. The times have changed. In recent years we have seen a proliferation of human development and "consciousness" programs, teaching skills for self-responsibility, meditation, intuitive development, non-manipulative communication, and other assets for enlightenment. There is a widespread popular interest today in such subjects in diverse sectors of the culture, including many people from the corporate sector and from government. Today we may have a "critical mass" of persons who have reached an evolutionary level where they are capable of and *will demand* more life-responsive forms of soTial organization.

Beyond Anarchy and Totalitarianism: "Cooperative Autonomy"

In the past, our experiments in social structure have tended toward anarchic freedom or totalitarian constraint. Both of these alternatives represent a distortion of the differentiation/integration balance required for organismic structure. In the totalitarian pattern, individual freedom and uniqueness are lost in "mass consciousness." In the anarchic pattern, there is a lack of integration within a higher-order context which could coordinate and give life meaning to the separate reaction against the tyranny of totalitarian control. (Note: the term "totalitarian" as used here transcends conventional political notions of "right" and "left," and may include much of what is considered "democratic" practice. It refers to a structure which violates the principle of free will, either directly through force or indirectly through manipulation.)

Today the time has come to consider an organismic alternative: that of cooperative autonomy. This paradigm is based on a different kind of order from the totalitarian order. It is based on the order of the living universe. An understanding of the principles of organismic order can give us a ground to stand on in building social forms for the future. Without this understanding, we risk being led by a legitimate fear of chaos to impose a totalitarian order which cuts off the life breath of the social structure.

Building an "Artificial Organism"

In considering how we might build organismic social structures, we are faced with the problem of creating an "artificial organism." A corporation or government is not a natural organism in the same sense as a human being. Clearly we will need some time to experiment with organismic social structures before we can answer with some degree of confidence questions such as what the "nervous system" and other essential "organs" of such a structure might be, and how to set up an "internal guidance system." Nonetheless, we can begin to look at some of the parameters that would be involved, building on the principles of organismic process that have been set forth in this paper. We have described an organismic structure as a self-organizing process in which the laws of creative synthesis provide the organizing principles. Such a process has the following properties:

1. intentionality, will, or purpose;
2. an organizing center (the "Creative Center" of the system) which is the agent of its intentionality;
3. "hierarchical heterarchy" — i.e., each level of the system is a "holon;"
4. "love" and "intelligence" (as defined in our postulates) as organizing principles of its intentionality;
5. dynamic equilibrium between the principles of differentiation and integration.

"Intentionality" of a Social Structure

The closest concept to organizational intentionality in current usage is that of the organization's "purpose" or "mission." However, in order for an organization to function as an organism, we must look beyond the sense in which these terms are generally used. The purpose of a "living" organization must be compatible for integration within the purpose of a higher-order organism. In this case the higher-order organism is the planet. (Of course, the lower-order purposes of sub-entities such as states and nations must also be considered. However, political and bureaucratic sub-entities at the present time are not organismically designed and are inadequate Creative Centers for planetary purpose.)

In order for an organization's purpose to be compatible for integration within the evolutionary purpose of the planet, it must consider the broader context within which it operates. Clearly, much of current attitude and practice within our collective life must be transformed to fulfill these conditions. Many of the behaviors of our political and economic institutions resemble the primitive defense mechanisms of immature organisms who have not yet discovered their Creative Center. They are based on fear and insecurity, on the belief that one must use force or manipulate in order to survive, on competition rather than cooperation, and on lack of trust in a supportive universe. Defensive patterns such as these spring from insecurity. They create an illusion of security, though it has no real foundation. In order to relinquish primitive defenses, we must discover the source of our only true security: cooperation with the evolutionary process and with the laws of creative synthesis which govern it. Both as individuals and as collective entities we need to make the fundamental discovery that the universe is a living process. The corollaries to this are: that the universe supports activity which is in harmony with these laws; and that it eventually destroys those patterns which oppose them. Thus, lifeless structures without will, heart, or true intelligence cannot undergo creative transformation.* They are doomed instead to violent shattering or a slow death by suffocation.

Some of the more obvious "counter-evolutionary" practices which have come to public attention are: rape and pillage of the environment; wasteful competitiveness; manipulative publicity; built-in obsolescence; energy inefficiency; the use of war and violence to obtain one's ends; insensitivity of organizations to the evolutionary needs of employees and of the public; calculation of the "bottom line" in terms of financial profit alone; and social injustice generally.

In addition to the more obvious scourges on our collective life, we must concern ourselves with the less apparent problems which derive from the lack or organismic structure and ideology in our collective institutions.

Let us return to the question of organizational purpose. If this purpose is compatible with universal principles, it will be a purpose which offers inspiration and life meaning to the persons associated with it. It will be a purpose which gives them a sense of participation in a larger purpose — a purpose which resonates with their own deepest human values. Thus it would inspire a level of commitment well beyond the motivating power of a paycheck alone. The most profound need of any human being is to feel that his or her life makes a difference in the world, in terms of intrinsic human values. Conversely, it is a basic human need to avoid participation in that which violates one's own standards of integrity. Participation in structures which violate fundamental values produces negative feedback from the participant's "internal guidance system." It can produce "dis-ease" at both physical and emotional levels, and is a major cause of stress and

---

*c.f. Ilya Prigogine's work on dissipative structures.

"demotivation" within our unhealthy social structures. It would surely bring a great release of commitment and creativity if we could learn to tape the deep human drive for life meaning and purpose. Yet, much of current management practice still relies on subtle manipulation by extrinsic reward rather than intrinsic motivation.

A corollary to aligning with a higher purpose is to make this purpose known to the participants in the organization. The purpose must be clearly articulated and communicated so that those who are joined as "co-creators" of the organization can be inspired and contribute their best efforts.

The "Creative Center" of an Organization

Now we need to ask, "How would such a purpose be formulated and by whom?" This is not an easy question to answer. As we have said, an organization is at best an "artificial organism." It may not have an obvious "Creative Center." A "Creative Center" would need to be identified or formed to function as the primary agent of intentionality within the organization. (Other lower-order "Creative Centers" could, of course, be established on the same principles.) It is likely that such a Center for a collective entity would best be formed by a group of persons. However, an individual with appropriate qualifications and counsel might, under certain circumstances, be the proper candidate for this role.

What would be the qualifications for membership in such a "steering council?" Most important would be the attunement of the members with cosmic order and with the organization's particular purpose within society. (Granted, this may not be simple to define.) Such persons would have a balanced development of the abstract and concrete mind, as well as the capacity to bridge between the two levels of mind. This would render them capable of grasping abstract organizing principles and of applying these in a practical way to the problems of the concrete world.

Attunement to the particular purpose of the organization would require an alignment of the will as well as certain kinds of knowledge. The person would need to feel "connected to" the particular purpose of the organization and feel an alignment of his or her individual purpose with that of the organization. The person would also need to be knowledgeable about the field of enterprise, its particular challenges, and how it interfaces with the broader environment. Such expertise would generally be more easily obtained with a team of people having complementary backgrounds. If a team approach were used, it would be desirable to balance other characteristics of the group members as well, so that requisise variety and complementarity in all relevant ways would be assured. In this way, each person could contribute a different piece to the total picture. (It seems premature to spell out what these characteristics would be. However, this might be a fertile field for management research in the future.) It would be important that the team members be strongly established in their sense of individual identity so that they do not fall prey to "group think." They need to be aware of their own biases, with the strengths and weaknesses inherent in them. And they must be able to detach themselves from their biases — even as they defend the values in them — so that they can appreciate the values in other perspectives. The team members will also need to be well-grounded in the principles of cooperation and creative synthesis so that they can seek the higher unity behind their divergent viewpoints.

Procedures Used by a Collective Creative Center

A Creative Center of this type would need to develop effective procedures to carry out its task. These would surely include some forms of conventional data-processing and decision-making — hopefully with the aid of an improved information system (to be discussed). In addition, communication with a higher-order Center would need to be established. The methods of invocation and evocation might serve as the basis for this. Experiment would have to reveal the most effective methodologies. We, as yet, have little experience with such procedures at a group level. Various techniques of group problem-solving such as "Synectics" and the brain-storming approach are already widely used in organizational settings. However, they lack certain organismic properties. Probably more relevant are the methods used for group discernment by certain spiritual communities such as Findhorn, the Quakers, and the Jesuit order. (It is an interesting fact that the field of spiritual discernment, out of fashion for some time, is recently attracting renewed interest in Church circles).

The same "caveats" which apply to individuals seeking higher-order guidance would, of course, apply to groups. Precautions would need to be taken to eliminate "noise" in the system, such as disruptive emotions and attachment to ideas and behaviors which are incompatible with organismic process. (This points to the need for certain personal characteristics in group members. These would include spiritual freedom, sensitivity to values, and an open mind.)

"Heterarchical Hierarchy" and Cooperative Autonomy

A living organization would have Creative Centers at the various organizational levels. They would be arranged as a "heterarchical hierarchy," with each sub-Center having its own domain of responsibility. The various levels and subdivisions within the organization, as well as the sub-entities — including the individuals — within these, would operate on the principle of cooperative autonomy. The differentiation principle would be respected at each level. Each unit — individual and collective — would thus feel the self-respect that comes from fulfilling a unique and necessary function within the whole.

Structuring "Organs" within an Artificial Organism

In order to achieve the goal of cooperative autonomy, it would be necessary in many cases to restructure the "organs" or sub-entities within the organization along more efficient and organismic lines. A notion borrowed from mathematics — that of "canonical functions" — is helpful here. The canonical functions of an entity are those which divide its tasks into subtasks such that no two subtasks overlap and that any given task can be accomplished by a combination of the subtasks. The well-known competition for "turf" among departments in an organization is largely a function of a non-canonical division of labor.

The "Nervous System" of an Organization

Another important requirement of organismic social structures is an information system with organismic properties. We now have the ability to construct the analogue of a nervous sytem in the form of distributed data processing. The popular notions about computers would make this seem unlikely. We live in a moment when computers seem to impose rigidity on office procedures. This rigidity is not a consequence of computers. It represents the failure of our own understanding in programming. Computer systems can be programmed to be adaptive and self-organizing. They could make diversity the rule rather than the exception.

Distributed data processing involves a system in which a multiplicity of (diverse) processors function together in a cooperative autonomy. Distributed data processing both provides a working model for developing our notions of organism and a method for implementing the nervous sytem of an artificial organism, such as a business. (Cf. Stafford Beers' *Brain of the Firm*)

The information processed by an artificial nervous system of this kind would include much of what is currently considered relevant "data." It would, in addition, include new forms of data which would be necessitated by the principle of "love" — the intrinsic valuing of the persons in the organization and the entities with which the organization interfaces in the environment. When employees are viewed as whole persons, much data of a "subjective" nature now become relevant — e.g., how people feel about their work and why, the quality of communications, etc.

Stress as "Information"

There is much information contained within "stress" — at individual and organization levels — that would be of great value to an organismic organization. Stress provides information about how human beings as total organisms are responding to a situation. There is thus a "holistic" quality to the information contained in stress that could be particularly useful for monitoring conditions which violate basic human needs. It could thus provide clues for redesign of the organization along more organismic lines. And it is precisely by learning how to turn information such as this to a creative purpose that we will begin to find out how to build organismic social structures in the concrete world. At the present time, this type of information is frequently wasted. Stress is often "managed" by relaxation programs or other forms of anesthetization rather than being considered as a sign of imbalance crying out for adjustment. The "demotivated" employee may be viewed as a misfit rather than as an indication that something may be lacking which she/he needs in order to feel inspired.

The Need for a Requisite Variety of Processors in an Information System

Our present data-processing systems frequently fail to consider the differing needs of various Creative Centers within the organization for particular types of information. Variables such as different requirements in terms of level of abstraction, time frame, etc. are not taken into account. Thus, many managers are frustrated by the piles of worthless paper on their desks and are handicapped in their decision-making by lack of relevant data. This is a major source of executive stress that could be significantly reduced by an organismic information system. A related need of organizations is to provide managers having differing kinds of responsibilities with specific training appropriate to their data handling needs. These needs, incidentally, will include more "people skills" in the organismic organization. When the "organs" or subentities of an organization are more canonically defined, this will give us clearer criteria for differentiating the classes of processors resquired within the overall information system.

Organismic communication seems to include another principle of organization in addition to that of heterarchical hierarch: that of direct communication of all parts of a system with all other parts. Such a process is suggested by research coming in from various sources such as studies of cellular communication, non-locality, holography, and the etheric web. As this principle applies to information flow within an organization, it suggests the need for communication channels going directly between any member of the organization and any other member. This could allow for appropriate information transfer under conditions when the usual channels would not serve the need. The notion that an invisible web of inter-connection may join all beings suggests the further possibility of making such a connection more visible. If people are joined in essence, acknowledgment of this inter-connection may play a vital role in their experience of life meaning. Business organizations often tend to view employees as role-defined commodities instead of in their wholeness. If the climate of work life could support people in relating to one another "from center to center" (a definition of love given by Teilhard), organizations could tap an enormous resource — the whole person. Perhaps we will find that love, or intrinsic valuation of persons, is a key to morale and productivity.

Building Learning into the System

Our postulates stated that learning is a fundamental aim in the living universe. This learning was said to be of a complex nature, involving dimensions of "will," "love," and "intelligence," and resulting in wisdom rather than mere knowledge. We have examined how cybernetic processes within a natural organism, the human being, enable it to learn from experience, to acquire wisdom, and to undergo creative transformation. Let us consider how some principles of learning at the individual level may apply to social structures.

Most organizations function in a manner which provides poor support for organismic learning. This applies both to the learning of individuals and to the learning of the organization as a collective entity. When learning does occur, it tends not to be the complex and multi-valued learning which results in true wisdom. Most organizations have little appreciation for wisdom. They often fail to recognize it, do not reward it, and have no procedures for storing it. An organismic organization would need to devise processes to support such learning.

These processes must be relevant to the various aspects of learning which our postulates refer to as will, love, and intelligence.

The "will" principle is related to qualities such as responsibility, focus, self-mastery, and initiatory/creative action. To support learning which involves the will, an organization must encourage self-responsibility and establish clear lines of accountability. People must learn skills of goal-setting, self-management, action-planning, and related areas which are pertinent to effective self-direction. The will principle is undermined when emergent purpose for the indiviudal is stifled in the name of organizational priorities. Thus, the growth needs and special gifts of employees must be considered as much as possible in job assignment to bring alignment of individual and organizational purpose.

Learning which involves the "love" principle develops one's capacity for right relations with oneself and others. A manager whose learning includes the "love" dimension can draw upon intrinsic motivation in the orchestration of human resources. She/he can be of service in evoking unified and committed efforts toward a common goal.

In considering the learning process as it involves the dimension of "intelligence," we are concerned primarily with organizing principles. Intelligence provides the means to effectively fulfill a given purpose through understanding the principles involved. It implies development of the abstract mind and the ability to relate abstract principles to concrete situations in a practical way. To support those aspects of learning based on intelligence, organizations must accord a more central role to the philosophical basis of their activity. They need to develop a coherent framework of principles — to be continuously updated — which describe the organization's mission and values as well as existing procedures for their implementation. In a company, this might be included in the policy manual, and could also be addressed in face to face situations. It is interesting to speculate on the possible effects of a reward system which could acknowledge contribution to organizational "intelligence." It might be that encouragement to reflect on principles and methods to enhance learning within the organization, would prove to be a powerful impetus to creativity and commitment. An organizational "philosophy of activity" could provide the rationale for such an approach.

A major factor which enters in to organizational learning, and cuts across all aspects of it, is the need to develop more constructive ways of viewing error and experiment. In organizations, as elsewhere in our culture, the concern for being right has severely undermined creativity. We need to encourage what Donald Michael, in *Learning to Plan and Planning to Learn,* has called the "new competency." The new competency includes the capacity to embrace error and to admit uncertainty. To develop this kind of competency, a climate must be created where people feel safe to acknowledge error and are supported in doing so. Procedures need to be established to extract the value from error, to understand what created it, and to reflect on how it might be avoided in the future. We also need to encourage thoughtful experiment, as progress occurs and living organisms learn through the creation of new forms.

Conclusion: The Bottom Line

In the living universe, the bottom line is measured by criteria more diverse than those commonly used in human institutions. These criteria derive from evolutionary purpose. They are concerned with the organism's ability to increase value (profit, order, syntropy) through creative synthesis. The viability of a structure, in the long run, is a function of that structure's alignment with evolutionary purpose, which includes its capacity to adapt to emergent processes within that purpose. As we seek to develop more organismic structures for human society, we will need to expand our conceptions of profit and the bottom line.

Notes

Assagioli, R. A., *Psychosynthesis, A Manual of Principles and Techniques* (New York: Hobbs, Dorman & Company, Inc.), 1965, (Baltimore: Penguin), 1976.

Assagioli, R. A. *The Act of Will* (Baltimore: Penguin), 1976.

Beers, S. *Brain of the Firm* (New York: Herder and Herder), 1972.

Burckhardt, T. *Alchemy: Science of the Cosmos, Science of the Soul* (London: Stuart and Watkins), 1967.

Crampton, Martha, "Psychosynthesis: Some Key Aspects of Theory and Practice." This is a chapter in *Innovative Psychotherapies,* ed. R. Corsini (New York: Wiley), In Press.

Gendlin, E. *Focusing* (New York: Everest House), 1978.

Green, E. and A., "On the Meaning of Transpersonal: Some Metaphysical Perspectives" *(Journal of Transpersonal Psychology,* Vol. III, No. 1), 1971.

Guenon, R., "La Grande Triade," *Revue De La Table Ronde,* 1936.

Hartshorne, C., *Creative Synthesis* (La Salle, Ill.: Carus Corporation).

Hirst, N., "Some Thoughts on Scientific Axiology: Its Metaphysical Basis and Prerequisite Variables," *Human Values and Natural Science,* Laszlo and Wilber, (eds.) (New York: Gordon and Breach), 1979.

Koestler, A., *Janus* (New York: Random House), 1978.

Koestler, A., *The Ghost in the Machine* (Chicago: Henry Regnery), 1967.

Michael, D., *Learning to Plan and Planning to Learn* (San Francisco: Jossey Bass), 1973.

Prigogine, I., "Order through fluctuation: self-organization and social system" in Jantsch, E. and Waddington, C. H. (eds.) *Evolution and Consciousness: Human Systems in Transition.* (Reading, MA.: Addison/Wesley, 1976).

Whitehead, A. N., *Process and Reality* (New York: MacMillan), 1929; (New York: Free Press), 1978.

Martha Crampton is a pioneer in the development of psychosynthesis in North America. She received an M.A. degree in Psychology from Bryn Mawr and studied with Robert Assagioli in Italy. She founded the Canadian Institute of Psychosynthesis in Montreal, which she directed for many years. In Montreal, she was a senior member of the Corporation of Psychologists of the Province of Quebec. Ms. Crampton is currently living in Redding, Connecticut, where, with Norman Hirst, she is cofounder of *Holodynamics,* an organization dedicated to research into life processes and to the fostering of creative synthesis in the various fields of human endeavor. Holodynamics offers counseling, educational and consulting services to individuals and to organizations.

>8<

PSYCHOLOGICAL THEORIES OF
HUMAN DEVELOPMENT:
LINKS TO THEOSOPHICAL CONCEPTS
Helen L. Bee

The field of psychology is extraordinarily diverse. Psychologists study human physiology, perception, learning, motivation, social interactions, development, personality, and emotional disturbance and therapy. In fact, different groups of people are involved in studying each of these aspects of human functioning, and I regret to say that we do not talk to each other very much, or read each other's papers. I know a little bit about each of these areas of research — mostly left over from my graduate school days — but I have little sense of the extent to which research in specialities other than my own has moved toward a more humanistic or theosophical view of man.

But I can speak for my own corner of the field, which is the study of human development. Until quite recently, I had spent most of my time thinking about, and doing research on, the development of children during the first 5 - 10 years of life. Like most developmental psychologists I had thought little about development over the full life-span, and not at all about the possible connections between life-span development and evolution in the theosophical sense.

My vision has broadened somewhat in the past year and a half, mostly because my publisher asked me to write a text on life-span development, which forced me to read and think in new ways. In the process, I have been quite startled to discover how close many new theories about adult development have come to the basic theosophical model of man and his evolution. What I want to do in these brief pages is to introduce some of those current theories and demonstrate how they may be linked to theosophical concepts.

Virtually all existing theories of development over a single life-span are *stage theories*. That is, they propose that each person passes through some definite series of steps or stages in progressing from birth to death. But there are at least three ideas about how those stages might be organized.

First, there are *maturational* stage theories. Theorists such as Arnold Gesell have argued that development has a fundamental biological underpinning; the different steps occur because of a fixed series of physical changes, a process psychologists call maturation. A baby must crawl before he can walk. A girl must begin menstruating before she can go through menopause, and so forth.

Theories like these are particularly relevant when we talk about the development of children; they are much less helpful when we try to consider the developmental patterns of adults. They are also much less clearly linked to theosophical concepts except for the basic assumption that the evolutionary process for each of us involves a series of distinct physical states, from mineral to vegetable to animal to human. One could argue that the maturational theories of development are merely extensions of this basic evolution into the single life-time. Still, I think this type of approach is of the least interest to theosophists.

A second type of theory, *sequential* theories, comes closer to theosophical thinking. Theories in this second group emphasize a series of age-linked stages defined by particular social roles or developmental tasks. Over a life-time, there are definable social and emotional tasks imposed on each of us. In childhood, for example, the child must learn basic skills such as reading and writing; in adolescence he must come to terms with new relationships with members of the opposite sex; as a young adult he must cope with the task of independence — of breaking away from the original family unit. Personal growth, in this view, results from successfully confronting and surmounting each of these tasks, in the correct sequence.

There are a number of sequential theories of development, two of which I find particularly interesting. First, there is an intriguing recent theory proposed by Daniel Levinson.

Levinson sees development as a series of alternating periods of relative stability, when a life structure is created, punctuated by periods of transition. During the transition phases, the individual reexamines the previous life-structure, decides what is worthwhile and what is not, and then creates a new pattern. Table 1 summarizes the major periods of stability and transition suggested by Levinson.

Thus far, Levinson has described the life course only for men, although he assumes that the same basic pattern of stable structure followed by transition characterizes the lives of women as well. Levinson is also very definite about the fact that he sees these alternating phases as "seasons" that follow one another irrevocably, but do not go anywhere in particular. That is, he does not see this whole process as consisting of growth or movement upward in any way.

On first inspection Levinson's model seems very untheosophical. Of all the life-span theories now being proposed, I have found it the least satisfying philosophically. But quite recently it struck me that in one sense, what Levinson is proposing is like a series of reincarnations *within* a given life-span. Each of us chooses a particular life structure — including family patterns, job, and relationships with other people. We live within the confines of that structure for a long time, learning what we can. But there comes a time when the structure "dies" — it ceases to satisfy our needs or we grow out of it in some sense. We then go through a period of questioning, of reevaluating the previous choices, of absorbing what we have learned in a conscious way, and deciding what is still to be done. Then we create a new structure, designed to meet our needs as we now see them.

We choose the pattern of physical existence each time. When we have learned what we have to learn in a given life,

Table 1

The major tasks of each developmental period, as proposed by Daniel Levinson.

Developmental period	Age	Tasks
EARLY ADULT TRANSITIONS	17 - 22	Terminate preadulthood; move out of preadult world and take preliminary steps into adult world; explore possibilities and make preliminary choices.
ENTERING THE ADULT WORLD	22 - 28	Create a first major life structure; usually marriage and a home of one's own occur; must explore options and create a stable life structure at the same time.
AGE THIRTY TRANSITION	28 - 33	Work on the flaws of the first life structure. Reconsider the choices of the early twenties, and make changes as needed.
SETTLING DOWN	33 - 40	Creat a major new life structure, more stable than the first one. Usually (among men, and nowdays many women) involves heavy commitment to work — to "making good" in an occupation. Often a "mentor" is involved, someone who guides and supports within the occupation.
MID-LIFE TRANSITION	40 - 45	Bridge from early to middle adulthood. Must reexamine the settling down structure and change or modify it. Focus is on "what have I done with my life?"
ENTERING MIDDLE ADULTHOOD	45 - 50	Create new life structure. Focus is on new relationships with children and on new occupational tasks, including serving as mentor to younger people.

The alternation of transitions and life structures is thought to continue until death, although Levinson does not specify the content of later transitions.

Adapted from Levinson, 1978

the life impulse fades and the physical body dies. Then there is a period of absorption of the lessons learned and finally another life-choice is made.

I was struck again by the cyclicity being described in both cases. If we put the two together, we find a series of mini-cycles within each life that are qualitatively similar to the larger cycles described by separate lives.

A second major sequential theorist is Erik Erikson. He was one of the first to propose a series of stages covering the entire life-span.

Erikson proposes that there are eight major stages, each one typified by a particular task or dilemma. I've summarized the eight stages, their tasks and the approximate ages at which the individual is thought to face each one, in Table 2. I should emphasize that these ages are definitely approximations. Erikson, like Levinson, thinks that the stages are partly, or largely, defined by the cultural expectations impinging on the individual. But in our culture, these are about the ages at which they occur.

Unlike Levinson, Erikson does not perceive the process as consisting of alternations of structure and transition. In Erikson's theory, each of the steps must be taken in turn and each builds upon the last. But because the steps are provoked by largely external demands, the individual has to face the next one whether he is finished with the previous one or not. A young adult must face the question of intimacy, for example, even if he has not yet fully handled the problem of identity. However, Erikson does believe that the success with which any one of us deals with a particular demxnd or dilemma depends on the completeness of our resolution of earlier dilemmas. Really healthy growth ending in genuine integrity rather than despair, requires that all of the prevous steps be handled successfully. If a child begins without basic trust, all the later tasks are that much more difficult.

Although Erikson's theory is sequential (rather than hierarchical, as we will see in a moment) he is nonetheless

The final group of developmental theories are *hierarchical*. In theories of this type, each succeeding stage grows logically out of the one before and you cannot move to the next step of the process until you have mastered the ones that came before. Sequential theories like Erikson's by contrast, describe a fixed series of tasks that come to you whether you are ready for them or not.

Hierarchical theories focus much more on inner processes than on external demands — on what each of us *does* with the demands, rather than on the demands or tasks themselves. Because of this emphasis on internal changes, I find the hierarchical theories to be the most theosophical. The image Leadbeater uses so often of each of us on a long ladder of personal development comes to mind. The rungs must be climbed one at a time, and new ones cannot be attempted until the current one is fully achieved. Furthermore, the steps in this process are internal changes, as each of us gradually comes in touch with his or her true nature, with the Self.

Hierarchical theories within developmental psychology do not have this larger evolutionary emphasis; only a single lifetime is described. But both the process of sequential steps, each growing out of what has gone before, and of increasing freedom from individual experience in each succeeding step, are built into these views.

The most notable hierarchical theory has been proposed by Jean Piaget, the Swiss psychologist. His central preoccupation has been with the development of thinking in children. He has said nothing about the development of adults, and little or nothing about any aspect of development other than cognitive. But his theory has been tremendously influential.

Essentially Piaget argues that mental development is a process of continuous *adaptation*. Our physical body adapts constantly to the demands on it — adjusting temperature, digesting food and so on — and so does the mind. Specifically, Piaget sees three aspects to adaptation: *assimilation, accomodation,* and *equilibration.* Assimilation is the process of taking in information, ideas, concepts, experiences. But we don't take things in exactly as they are. Rather, as we take them in we fit them into some existing system, some prior concept or model.

For example, suppose you ask a friend when her birthday is. She says December 25. That's a straightforward piece of information, but what you do with it — what structure you assimilate it to, in Piaget's terminology — depends on the set of concepts and theories you have developed for yourself. If you are an astrologer, you may say "Oh, a Sagittarius!" and

Table 2

The eight stages of development proposed by Erik Erikson.

Period	Age	Tasks
1	0 - 1	Basic trust vs. mistrust. Baby must come to believe in the regularity of her environment, and that she can affect it.
2	2 - 3	Autonomy vs. shame, doubt. Child can now move around and wants to be more independent; risk is that he may develop shame or doubt about his new skills if he is not successful or if his parents do not support his explorations.
3	4 - 5	Initiative vs. guilt. The child strikes out on her own still more, trying out new skills. Child becomes more forceful, more aggressive. But if she goes too far, she may experience guilt.
4	6 - 12	Industry vs. inferiority. The school-age child must cope with the demands of school tasks — reading, writing, arithmetic and all the rest. The risk is that he will fail and feel inferior.
5	13 - 18	Identity vs. role confusion. The teenager must develop a new sexual identity and an occupational identity; who am I as a man or a woman and what will I do with my life? If these tasks are not dealt with, the risk is confusion.
6	19-25	Intimacy vs. isolation. The young adult must enter into a genuinely intimate relationship in which the individuality is partly submerged. If this cannot be achieved, the risk is isolation.
7	26-40 +	Generativity vs. stagnation. The adult must find satisfaction through use of her mental talents (in a job), creative abilities, or rearing of children. If satisfaction is not achieved, the risk is a sense of stagnation.
8	40 +	Ego integrity vs. despair. The older adult must put all the experiences of life together and try to understand what it all has meant, to achieve a sense of an integrated self, and accept whatever he has become. If this is not accomplished, the risk is a sense of despair.

Adapted from Erikson, 1963

store the information that way. If you are a Christian, you may say "Oh, on Christmas!" and associate an entirely different set of ideas with that birthdate. Someone else who is neither an astrologer nor a Christian may associate the date with winter or with the winter solstice or equivalent. If the listener lived in the northern part of Norway, December 25 occurs just at the time when total darkness descends for several weeks and that may be the set of ideas to which the information is assimilated.

The basic point is that although assimilation is going on all the time, we do not just assimilate facts or experiences in some neutral way. We change them as we take them in.

The complementary process in Piaget's theory is accommodation. This is the process of internal change that takes place because of the new information or new experience. We change things as we absorb them, but we are changed too, in the process. Our ideas change when we hear new facts; our skills change as we practice them; your ideas and understanding of development psychology are changing — accommodating as you read these words.

The third basic process Piaget proposes is the balancing act between assimilation and accommodation, called equilibration. Piaget argues that over the period of childhood, the infant, toddler, preschooler, and later the school child develops a series of structures — models of the world if you will — as a result of all her assimilating and accommodating. Each of these new structures, new models, represents an equilibrium. But new experiences keep throwing the thing off balance, since the model does not handle everything. So the old model breaks down and a new model has to be built up again. In this view, development is punctuated by periods of disequilibrium, when the child gives up an old way of viewing things and then must struggle to find a new way. Each succeeding structure, or model, is built on what went before and they must be created in a logical order. The child must understand what adding and subtracting means before he can grasp multiplication; he must also understand inductive logic before deductive logic is possible.

Obviously this bears a distinct resemblance to what Levinson has proposed, except that Piaget is talking about *inner* changes and Levinson more about external ones. In addition,

Piaget is quite definite about the fact that one must complete a given phase before going on to the next — like building a pyramid. In contrast, Levinson assumes that some of the transition points are triggered by changes in external circumstances, such as the death of a parent or the loss of a job or children leaving home. Still, despite the differences, I think that one can superimpose a hierarchical view onto Levinson's theory and approach a view of life-span development that is close to what many of us actually experience in our own inner ("spiritual") growth.

Patricia Sun, a spritual teacher on the West Coast, once likened this process to a series of boxes. Each of us builds a box to live in, made up of our ideas about ourself, about our strengths and limitations. But eventually the box becomes a too-tight fit; we find ourselves restricted by the box we have created. At some point, part of the box (or the whole thing) must be knocked down so that there is more room. For a short while we feel euphoric. Free at last! But we have simply built a larger box, and that box too must be knocked down in its turn at some later point. Each of the periods when we have a large-enough-for-now-box is a kind of equilibrium or "life structure." But we continue to assimilate and accommodate — to grow, if you will — and eventually we must throw out that equilibration and search for another.

On the surface, then, Piaget's hierarchical model of development fits well with theosophical (and related) concepts of personal evolution. But I don't want to take the linkgages too far. It is not clear to me from any of the theosophical literature, nor from the writings of other teachers, that the steps on the ladder (or the series of Patricia Sun's boxes) must necessarily be accomplished in precisely the same sequence by everyone. We are all going in the same direction, but unlike Piaget's theory, in which there is a single path proposed, in theosophical writings there are many orders in which understanding may be achieved — at least at the lowly levels at which most of us function! One person may develop the mind but be lacking in compassion; another may have developed those two aspects in the other order. So although the process of equilibration from developmental theory may be a reasonable match to theosophical views, the sequential aspect of the process is more clear when we study the development of children's thinking than when we look at individual experiences of spiritual growth.

Despite these differences, however, I am increasingly struck by important parallels between the current thinking about development in an individual lifetime, and theosophical views of evolution over many lifetimes. Theorists such as Erikson or Roger Gould (another hierarchical theorist) see a significant transition at mid-life, when many of us turn inward and attempt to shed the patterns of the particular personality (to use the theosophical language). We try to understand who we are, where we have been, and what it means. We try to develop unexplored and underdeveloped parts of ourselves. There is a strong sense of personal growth in these theories. Living is not just passing time. There is movement, direction, increasing integration. As Roger Gould puts it:

> As our life experience builds, ideally we abandon unwarranted expectations, rigid rules and inflexible roles. We come to be the owners of our own selves, with a fuller, more independent adult consciousness . . . . We come to accept that we own only ourselves. No one else owes us love, attention, admiration, or anything else. We are no longer dependent, powerless children, and we can now view life from the independent vista of adulthood. (Gould, 1978, p. 21).

This hopeful view of man, with emphasis on inner change, marks a shift within psychology away from mechanistic theories of development and learning, toward more humanistic views. Each step in this direction moves the field closer to the theosophical model of man.

References

Those of you who are interested in this area may find any of the following books intrguing. I am especially fond of Vaillant's book, despite its Freudian orientation. Gould's is also extremely interesting.

E. H. Erikson, *Childhood and Society*. (New York: Norton, 1950, 1963), (Available in paperback).

R. Gould, *Transformations: Growth and Change in Adult Life*. (New York: Simon & Schuster, 1978).

D. J. Levinson, *The Seasons of Man's Life*. (New York: Knopf, 1978), (Available in paperback).

G. E. Vaillant, *Adaptation to Life: How the Best and the Brightest Come of Age*. (Boston: Little, Brown, 1977), (Available in paperback).

Helen Bee, Ph.D., taught at Clark University (Worcester, Massachusetts) and the University of Washington. She is now doing research part-time at the University of Washington, and spends the rest of her time writing. Dr. Bee has four texts on the market, including *The Developing Person* (Harper & Row, 1980), *Invitation to Psychology* (Academic Press, 1979), and *The Developing Child* (Harper & Row, 1978). This article appeared in the *American Theosophist*, 1980 Special Spring issue.

⟩9⟨

CONVERGENCE OF THE TWAIN:
MODERN PSYCHOLOGY AND
THEOSOPHIC THOUGHT
Vern Haddick

Alien they seemed to be:
No mortal eye could see
The intimate welding of their later history.

Or sign that they were bent
By paths coincident
On being anon twain halves of one august event.

Till the Spinner of the Years
Said "Now!" And each one hears,
And consummation comes, and jars two hemispheres.

— *Thomas Hardy*

When the Theosophical Society was founded a century ago, psychology and the perennial wisdom, which H. P. Blavatsky and H. S. Olcott hoped to revitalize in the modern world, seemed as far apart as the iceberg and The Titanic of Hardy's poem. Yet their paths also, like those of the poet's twain, are proving coincident, and the "now" of their full encounter is becoming more and more likely.

124

During the eighteen eighties Western psychology was concerned chiefly with laboratory studies of sensation and perception. Such major figures as Hermann Helmholtz and Wilhelm Wundt dominated the field and analyzed mental phenomena into the simplest possible units, attempting to demonstrate how neurological processes underlay all mental functions. However, as Blavatsky wrote with so much energy at the time, this focus was not productive; it represented only a temporary eddy counter to the stream of emergent holistic understanding. According to her the laws upon which human existence and behavior rest are of another sort, such as:

> The fundamental identity of all Souls with the Universal Over-Soul...and the obligatory pilgrimage for every Soul...through the Cycle of Incarnation (or "Necessity") in accordance with Cyclic and Karmic law. (*The Secret Doctrine*, I, p. 17)

Therefore until her death in 1891 she continued to denounce the limited physiological and materialistic orientation of the new science, and she supported as she could the first questionings by some psychologists, such as George T. Ladd of Yale University, of a few premises of the late nineteenth century science. Still her ideas, which might have been useful in designing a metaphysically-based psychology, were ahead of their time, and they remained either unknown or rejected by the academic psychologists of the day.

At the turn of the twentieth century the situation was essentially unchanged. In 1900 Sigmund Freud published his first major work, *The Interpretation of Dreams,* and for six decades his theories provided the framework around which modern depth psychology and psychotherapy were constructed. Freud's assumptions were still those of a materialistic science, and upon them he sought to build a model of the mind which could account for the psychological phenomena he observed within himself and his patients. Although he saw only a fragment of the whole picture, he extended it beyond the range of conscious phenomena studied by previous experimental psychologists, and he established the premise that primary mental activities are unconscious, even while, like conscious processes, they operate according to the rules of mechanistic causality.

While Freud's contributions incorporated the materialistic assumptions held widely during his time, a few contemporary psychical researchers and pioneer investigators of mystical states of consciousness were opening themselves to ideas from the perennial wisdom such as Blavatsky was attempting to disseminate. Several even acknowledged their theosophical connections. F. W. H. Myers and Richard Bucke, who wrote important early volumes on parapsychology and mysticism, had studied Theosophy; and Edward Carpenter, who conducted pioneer investigations into mystical states of consciousness, sometimes lectured for theosophical lodges. William James, often called the father of American psychology, wrote not only a best-selling textbook on *The Principles of Psychology* but another on *The Varieties of Religious Experience* in which he quoted from Blavatsky's *The Voice of the Silence*. In both works James concluded that psychology is an unsystematic and incomplete science, or perhaps no science at all, since the undeniable evidence of his and others personal, subjective experience demonstrated the effects of indeterminate, unpredictable free will and choice — a view already expressed by Blavatsky in such statements as:

> There is a divine power in every man which is to rule his life, and which no one can influence for evil, not even the greatest magician. Let men bring their lives under its guidance, and they have nothing to fear from man or devil. (*Dynamics of the Psychic World,* p. 29)

Within the theosophical movement itself, during the first years of the new century, momentum toward developing a broadly based psychology received new power from three books by Annie Besant. Her *A Study of Consciousness, Theosophy and the New Psychology,* and *Thought Power* soon became recognized as classic early studies of the dimensions of consciousness. A couple of decades later Krishnamurti's discussions of conditioning and consciousness opened another provocative area for psychological investigation and began to influence some key theosophical writers, even though orthodox psychologists did not make much use of his insights. Yet while such topics remained beyond the pale for most traditional practitioners, they had impact upon the general public, and they well may have influenced such ground-breaking depth psychologists of the new generation as Carl Jung and Roberto Assagioli. Even though after the death of William James academic psychologists and the psychoanalytic establishment held to their mechanistic, materialistic assumptions, Jung began to widen understanding of the unconscious to incorporate a collective dimension, and Assagioli discussed quite openly a "higher unconscious" with possibilities for rich creative development and a "transpersonal Self" that can serve as a focus for relating the personality to an evolutionary process that moves from fragmentation toward wholeness, inclusiveness, and unity. Such recognition of possibilities as potential realities for the future, not just fantasies, paralleled insights of Blavatsky and Besant, to mention only two theosophical writers who had already discussed the issues of karma, insight, and choice so lucidly.

But for a while longer, even after Abraham Maslow organized humanistic psychology in 1963 as an umbrella movement in which existentialists, client-centered therapists, and others could study previously ignored human potentials, the majority of professional psychologists were not yet ready to consider mystical and metaphysical views of human consciousness. That reluctance began to melt toward the end of the sixties, when the growth movement in psychology came into its own. Then the works of such innovators as Otto Rank, Assagioli, Ira Progoff, and Martha Crampton popularized the view that obstructions to self-unfoldment represent resistances to the onward flow of experience, which constantly attempts to overcome such blocks by new "encounters of the spirit," new intuitive and symbolic breakthroughs which then can be related back to the individual's daily life. The transpersonal psychology movement launched in 1969 brought together a number of behavioral scientists, therapists, and educators to research and integrate parapsychology, the psychology of spiritual practice, East-West psychology, and such psycho-spiritual approaches to therapy as Psychosynthesis. Thus a professional forum was provided where insights of the theosophic tradition could be related to the more advanced work in modern depth psychology, if scholars and practitioners were willing to cultivate the necessary expertise in both fields. Thus when members of both groups are now equally appreciative of such books as Ken Wilber's *The Spectrum of Consciousness* and Huston Smith's *The Forgotten Truth,* and when some educators and psychologists are seeking to infuse the new holistic psychologies with aspects of the perennial wisdom, convergence at least of segments of modern psychology and theosophic thought seems a near reality.

The Theosophic tradition attests that throughout history many individuals have been concerned with impulses and growth toward more inclusive consciousness. In the modern world it has taken at least a century for psychologists as a group to develop such a concern. However, interest in finding ways to build the processes of illumination, mystical union, transcendence, and cosmic unity into formal and informal healing relationships is at last a recognizable part of the scene. At the present time several professors and students in the psychology programs at the California Institute of Asian Studies in San Francisco, under the guidance of Dr. Paul E. Herman in a theosophic therapy project funded in part by the Kern Foundation, are exploring the interface between modern theosophy and twentieth century depth psychology, seeking to formulate a distinctive theory and practice of therapy based upon the perennial wisdom. They have found particularly helpful the earlier explorations by Laurence and Phoebe Bendit and other members of the Theosophical Research Centre in London.

Until the present time the theosophical movement has not developed anything really equivalent to modern depth psychology. The contribution of the perennial wisdom has been strongest in the realm of philosophy or metaphysics, of exploring the ultimate source of all existence and the evolutionary pattern of cosmic process. On the other hand, during most of its hundred years of independent development Western psychology has been predominantly a science of phenomena, not of states of awareness, a quest for techniques of doing, not for relating holistically to Self and environment. Yet as modern depth psychology has evolved, such practitioners as Jung, Rank, Assagioli, Progoff, and certain transpersonal psychologists have found that the human being, through direct experience of his basic spiritual nature, can activate resources and creativity of a magnitude not previously suspected. Thus they have brought modern psychology into position to dialogue fruitfully with the perennial wisdom. They have also developed practical means to help make certain aspects of theosophical thought experientially available to a more general audience than in the past. On its side the theosophic tradition remains highly qualified to furnish the modern world ever-fresh restatements of "the oldest philosophy . . . the inheritance of all nations" (John B. S. Coats in the Foreword to *The Universal Flame*). Out of their convergence theosophy and depth psychology need to produce, and disseminate to the whole network of informal and formal helping relationships, which are such an important part of the contemporary scene, ways of working with the higher energies that can move us forward to the next stage of our growth. Even though it is probably true, as Laurence Bendit speculated, that healing and growth are processes "taking place entirely within the mind of the patient" and that "the mind of the analyst acts as the catalyst . . . [for] the release of energies hitherto held in check or prevented from expressing themselves in normal ways" (*An Introduction to the Study of Analytical Psychology,* p. 11), theosophy shows that the available energies are much more extensive than modern psychology has realized and that new ways for working with them are still to be devised. Blavatsky had in mind such greater energies, and approaches to working with them, when she wrote passages like the following:

> This *thinking of oneself* as this, that, or the other, is the chief factor in the production of every kind of psychic or even physical phenomena. (*Dynamics of the Psychic World,* p. 11)

and

> There is another kind of prayer; we call it *will-prayer,* and it is rather an internal command than a petition. When we pray we pray to "our Father in Heaven" — in its esoteric meaning . . . . Prayer is an occult process bringing about physical results. Will-power becomes a living power. (*The Key to Theosophy,* pp. 25-26).

129

The energy of altruistic love, so closely associated with the first objective of the Theosophical Society, is another such area for joint work which the perennial wisdom can help rescue from the neglect it has suffered to date at the hands of modern psychology.

Within the last few years Progoff has written of these matters from the point of view of his depth psychology; as he stated, "The meaning and goal of man's life is that he fulfill within himself the potentialities of existence that are present in the seed of his organic nature" (*Depth Psychology and Modern Man*, p. 252). From such a perspective it becomes the task of a holistic therapy to incorporate knowledge of the principles of spiritual growth that operate in the human being, to the fullest extent that the traditions and special circumstances of culture and history of the time allow.

People seek therapy or other varieties of help when something is not working well in their lives and they have not been successful in their efforts to find answers or to change things for the better. An effective therapy must help them to examine old beliefs about themselves and the world, and to try out new ways to conceive of themselves, other persons, their situation, and their environment. In other words, they need help to transcend their limiting beliefs and to become capable of having those experiences which can make life fuller and more complete. In this sense true help both restores the client's sense of wholeness within himself and enlarges his sense of relationship to the rest of life. Here again modern psychology, as it has developed from Freud's vision of integrating repressed wishes into the domain of conscious life, to Progoff's connecting the person through "vital experience" to the seed-potentials of his nature, coincides with the wisdom that theosophy has carried forward through the ages; and the two disciplines share common ground for further work together.

Some insights into how to bring about his larger integration were given within the modern theosophical movement at least as early as Besant's *Talks with a Class*. In that book she emphasized several principles for transmuting the passions of the individual personality into vehicles for further development. She felt that, first, the science of spirituality is the science of realizing personal, collective, and cosmic oneness experientially; second, the process of spiritual development requires the concentration of one's consciousness on enduring, unitive planes of being; and third, since in the natural evolutionary process energy is passed down from the enduring Self into the personality, as a means of gaining experience in the physical realm, the wise procedure is to cultivate spiritual transmutation in a manner which does not violate the individual unnecessarily from fellow beings.

Since all life which pervades the universe is ultimately one, the restoration or fostering of larger life within an individual is a "permissive, not an active" process. Laurence Bendit continues:

> Whatever the external methods used, whether psychological, chemical (pills or medicine) or manipulative, nobody and nothing heals a person otherwise than by releasing the things which have prevented him from healing himself. (*The Mysteries Today,* p. 27)

Such an orientation recognizes that throughout the universe life is guided and develops "from within outward." The inner Self represents a pull of the future toward which the path of growth leads. The clearest representation of what is yet to be achieved is found within the individual, and it must be respected and loved as a unique spark of the Being which encompasses all individuals. This recognition has been stated in another way in *The Mystery of Healing,* produced by The Medical Group, the Theosophical Research Centre, London:

> Normal health may be said to be present when a person is at peace with himself and in a harmonious relationship with his whole environment. (p. 6)

The right relationship to one's experience can vary widely from day to day, and from one period of life to another, because it represents the series of successive adjustments which make up the growth process, understood in its widest terms. According to both the perennial wisdom and the findings of Rank, Assagioli, Progoff, and other modern psychologists, harmonious interaction between parts, whether of an individual, a family or group, or the whole universe, rests upon a foundation of acceptance and love. The Eastern outlooks on life, such as Taoism, Buddhism, and some of the Hindu philosophies, have for a long time fostered a willingness to accept and love things more or less as they are, as sufficiently complete in themselves. However, this has not been the case in the West. Yet recent developments in depth psychology are indicating that a person lives more satisfactorily, more aesthetically, even under conditions of great surface tension, when more levels of his being, and especially the deepest levels, are quiet, accepting, and loving. This tardy convergence of the two traditions at the point of dynamic stillness and love illuminates another element important to a distinctive theosophic theory and practice of therapy. Real help must provide ways to understand, accept, love, and integrate the various parts of oneself, as well as the parts of larger surrounding worlds.

Modern psychology has produced many studies of the aggressive, competitive, violent impulses in human beings but almost no research into the power of love. The sociologist Pitirim Sorokin at Harvard University made some beginning investigations into the subject of creative altruism after the Second World War, but according to Dr. Tom Tutko of San Jose State University, in California, except for his own research the subject of loving and appreciative behavior is almost totally ignored by other scholars at the present time. Theosophy carries forward the long tradition of metaphysical knowledge that all life is one and that universal brotherhood is a value worthy of intense cultivation. These truths may well be its most valuable gift to modern psychology today.

In his book *Self Knowledge: a Yoga for the West* Laurence Bendit has sketched a model consisting of elements from Western psychology and Eastern thought, for a theosophic program of self-development. It involves gaining experience on four levels of fresh perception, each of which opens out a wider gestalt that can become the arena for more integrated living with oneself, one's fellows, and ultimately the whole of reality. The successive stages might for convenience be called "catharsis," "active imagination," "passive alertness," and "approach to Being." Yet merely naming or describing them is not really helpful, as both the theosophic tradition and modern psychology have pointed out. It is necessary for the person, whether working alone or with another, to translate them into immediate experiences at each level.

The following exercise, using Bendit's model, has been developed from work in the Theosophic Therapy Project at the California Institute for Asian Studies as an illustration of how elements of modern psychology and the perennial wisdom can be brought together to translate such a key therapeutic concept as altruistic love into experiential terms, suitable for using in one's own inner work, with a client, or in a group setting.

You may find it a challenge to try this exercise by yourself, with another person, or in a group setting, and see how it opens for you possibilities for new understanding and growth.

An Exercise to Explore the Energy of Love

1. Sit comfortably and close the eyes. Become aware of the breath passing in and out of the body. As you breathe, take a breath and when you exhale say to yourself the word "Relax." Each time you say "Relax" to yourself feel it taking effect on the various parts of the body, the head and face, the shoulders, the trunk, the arms and legs, the feet. Then turn attention to the thought process, and as you say "Relax" feel it clearing and limbering up the mind. Proceed the same way with the feelings, letting go of any tensions there, and clearing yourself of any emotional concerns. Now, as you experience the body, the thought process, and the feelings as a unit, relaxed and comfortable, see if that unity can tell you anything about the role that love, or love-energy has played in your life as a whole.

2. Still sitting comfortably with your eyes closed, as a unity of relaxed, alert body, feelings, and mind, imagine yourself in a natural setting that you find attractive, warm, and serene. You are in a sunny meadow which you are going to walk slowly across to climb the gentle incline to the top of a hill on the other side. As you make the crossing during the next few minutes, and climb the hill, review in backward-sequence the chief events of your life, from where you are just now, to what you did earlier in the day, to what you did yesterday, and so back to the earliest time you can remember. In this review let your attention focus on the role that love, or love-energy, has played in each segment of your life that you consider. What have your experiences of love been like? What have you brought to each of them, and taken away?

3. In the review as you get back near the time of your birth, you approach the top of the hill. Up there ahead of you, you become aware of a bluish-white glow which moves forward to meet you. There is nothing threatening about it or the experience. As the glow comes near you see that it is actually a person or other friendly being. You become aware of details of its appearance, and you realize it is your Wise Person; it is the resource for the clearest wisdom available to you. You stand face-to-face there in the sunlight on the top of the hill, and the Wise Person begins to speak with you about the purpose and meaning and possibilities of love in your life, both in the past and in the future. Take time to allow the discussion to proceed as far as it can; ask whatever questions you need to of the Wise Person; get in touch as fully as you can with the message about love, and the energy of love, which the Wise Person shares with you.

4. When the dialogue with the Wise Person has run its course, you turn aside and start to descend the hill again. As you walk slowly back toward the meadow you review the chief events of your life in proper chronological order this time, beginning with early childhood and coming forward. Being fully aware of the message about love, and the energy of love, which the Wise Person has shared with you, you focus your attention on the pattern that the love energy has assumed in expressing itself in your life to date. How has that purpose been playing itself out through you? How have you been cooperating with, and interfering with it? What changes would you make, in light of what the Wise Person has told you about love and love-energy?

5. By the time you reach the center of the meadow again, you have come back to the present time in reviewing the way the purpose of your particular love-energy has been expressing itself through your life. As you get to your original starting place, you meet the Wise Person there already. Take another few minutes to ask the Wise Person any further questions you may have about the purpose, meaning, and possibilities of love in your life. Speak briefly about the next developments in the unfolding of that process in your life, as you have come to understand it. What things can you do to cooperate with that purpose? Do you choose to undertake them? In bringing the experience to a close you may want to say something about these issues to the Wise Person, while he bids you goodbye.

6. When the experience has completed itself, breathe deeply several times to relax your body, feelings, and mind again; then slowly open your eyes and record or share with another person several of the things that you gained from the exercise.

Vern Haddick received his graduate education at the University of California, Berkeley, and Columbia University. He is Associate Professor of Integral Counseling Psychology and a member of the Theosophic Therapy Research Project at the California Institute of Asian Studies in San Fransisco.
This article was published in the Special Spring issue, 1980, of the *American Theosophist.*

THE NEED FOR A MULTI-LEVEL, PROCESS-ORIENTED PSYCHOLOGY
Dane Rudhyar

What is now taught as psychology in universities are the various attempts, classified in a number of "schools," to use the scientific method of observation, generalization, system-building, experimentation, and testing in order to interpret and explain a specific type of phenomena. These phenomena refer to what is broadly and imprecisely called "consciousness," and to the manner in which this consciousness is involved in, and often dictates — or seems to dictate — human activity or behavior.

In ancient times — and for the traditional college-trained person this almost exclusively means in the Greece of Plato, Aristotle and their followers — psychology was part of philosophy. Philosophy included or was the foundation for most types of knowledge, what we call physics and related sciences today being then seen as "natural philosophy." Psychology was thus the part of philosophy which referred specifically to consciousness or to self-knowledge. The well-known inscription at Delphi enjoined man to know himself. Knowledge is the formalized result of consciousness, the formalizing or formulating agent being what we call "the mind." The great problem was how to define that which is conscious, the knower. That was called the Soul, which in Greek philosophy had two main aspects: *psyche,* that which experiences feelings or emotions, and *nous,* the rational being able to function in the realm of Ideas or Archetypes.

Greek philosophy used mainly a deductive type of thinking, starting from great ideas or principles of being. Modern psychology instead is essentially empirical in its approach. Even psychologists like C. G. Jung and Abraham Maslow who were not afraid to deal with subjectivity and introspection insisted on retaining the empirical methods of modern science. They *had to* do so in order not to cut themselves off entirely from what now is considered the mainstream of Western civilization, at least since the Renaissance and Francis Bacon.

Empirical knowledge is objective knowledge. The basic issue is, however, what is to be considered an object of knowledge. For the post-Renaissance Euro-American scientist, objectivity refers to what can be perceived by the senses and the modern instruments immensely extending the scope of sense-perceptions. These perceptions, moreover, in order to be acceptable to science, have to be obtained under strict experimental conditions. They must be repeatable by any trained observer. They must also be measurable and definable in terms of some kind of activity, that is of observable and recordable changes. Thus the field of scientifically objective knowledge finds itself limited by these conditions. It may be so limited as to lose all meaning in some directions. As Einstein once said, the physicist comes to know more and more about less and less.

Subjective knowledge, in contrast, is knowledge which does not depend primarily on sense-data, though sense reactions may be involved in a subjective experience. Subjective experiences may not be repeatable, and they usually cannot be measured in precise quantitative terms. Nor can they be recorded in a *direct* manner. The mind may seem able to record the *experience,* but what is recorded in words is the mind's *interpretation* of it, and this interpretative record is most often made *after* the subjective experience. The mind thus gives a kind of objectivity to the subjective experience. People who insist on the validity of subjective experiences tend to give much too little consideration to what is involved in the objectivating activity of the mind. A great deal is involved: the entire sociocultural background of the interpreting mind is involved, the state of the whole culture of the experiencer is involved, and the state of the whole of humanity and the planet Earth is involved.

The empirical and objective knowledge sought and obtained by modern science is, however, also affected by the state of the scientist's culture and by the level the evolution of mankind has reached when the knowledge is obtained. The belief that laws of nature and universal constants are not affected by the state of evolution of the universe is an unprovable assumption. It could well be as much in error as would be the belief that all the functions of a human body operate in exactly the same manner whether the body is one year, thirty years, or eighty years old. Such beliefs give to the factor of time a strictly neutral character: time is considered as an abstract dimension along which measurements can be made by clocks, just as length, height, and breadth are measured by yardsticks or more sophisticated instruments. This, however, is not the only way one can conceive of time. Another conception of it could, as we will presently see, provide a foundation for the development of a psychology very different from the present scientific type, as well as an equally different approach to the place of man in the universe.

In the past, scientists believed that matter was solid and changed only by the action of external forces like wind, rain or sunshine. But today physicists speak, for example, of the half-life of atomic disintegration, thus of an internal process of a very complex nature. Similarly, psychologists once spoke of soul, mind, reason, will, and intelligence as if they were, if not entities, at least set characteristics of a well-defined person whose essential identity was unquestioned, even though this identity was constantly challenged and perhaps severely undermined by the forces of human nature. But today these components of the inner life and experience of human beings have lost much, if not most, of their relatively set and definite character. The inner life of a human being is now seen to be as much an unceasing series of complex changes as the everyday outer existence of a city-dweller engaged in a variety of social, cultural, and business pursuits.

Academically-oriented psychologists today are concerned most of the time with this human nature and the way it operates, thus with either human behavior in general, or the behavior of brain, nerves, and cells when actions and reactions that can be called psychological occur. But a large minority of psychologists, whose activities are widely publicized and attract people of all types, are instead primarily concerned with the psychological welfare and the problems, not only of objective behavior, but also of subjective consciousness which distress, confuse or impede individuals. Psychology can therefore be mainly descriptive of objective sequences of scientifically measurable events, or it can primarily aim at the cure of psychomental disturbances or the removal of emotional and intellectual blockages. In the first case psychology is one natural science among many; it is closely linked with physics and chemistry. In the second case it becomes psychotherapy, and in more specific and extreme instances, psychiatry — a branch of medicine.

In this second case, psychotherapeutic practices may be used to help individuals, who may be considered "normal," to develop to a far greater degree their potential of growth and self-fulfillment. Then psychology not only becomes the foundation of various kinds of psychotherapy, but it finds itself involved in religious and philosophical issues. These issues are inevitably and indissolubly associated with, and indeed the products of, the particular character of our society.

Society is today unquestionably in a state of acute and world-wide crisis. This social, cultural, political, and religious upheaval can be interpreted as a crisis of radical collective transformation. But the activities and the consciousness of the persons living in such a tumultuous society are not only conditioned by the collective crisis; in many cases the crisis becomes focused as their own psychological crisis. As individuals succeed in transforming their personalities and dealing with the stresses and perversions family, school, and society have imposed upon them, they become focal points for the collective transformation, centers of radiation for new values. But by what process can they reach such a state? This becomes the crucial question for those individuals who seek to meet their crises of transformation not in a kind of lonely vacuum, but in terms of participation in a process that involves the whole of mankind — a planetary process.

When we speak of process we necessarily imply time. Time, however, is not merely the tic-toc-ing of a clock marking a series of measurable units as abstract as numbers 1, 2, 3, 4, etc. Time can be understood and experienced as *the process of transformation itself.* In other words, the process does not occur *in* time; it *is* time. Once we realize this, the next realization is that time operates in terms of cycles: Time itself has a cyclic structure.

Instead of the word, time, we could use "change." Change is not one-directional. It operates in basically repetitive patterns. Experiences recur. Sunrise, and spring, birthing and dying recur. They do so rhythmically, cyclically. Nevertheless, the rhythms of existence are extemely complex. A multitude of factors are involved, and each factor is related to all the others. Processes of change and transformation also take place at several levels of being — that is, of activity and consciousness — all of which interact. A process of human transformation should therefore be understood in terms of a philosophy of cycles and in terms of the realization that a human being *can* function at several levels of activity and consciousness. What is at stake is not merely personal growth — the narrowly emphasized ideal of our present-day Human Potential Movement — but a process of transformation whose meaning can only be understood in terms of the cyclic development of Humanity-as-a-whole and also of the entire earth.

Such a development occurs through successive transitions (or passages) from one level to the next. At each level, a centralizing factor operates, around which the development of increasingly complex experiences and relationships becomes organized. Any radical transition from one level to another leads to the raising of the centralizing factor to the new level. This level indicates not only a quantitatively more inclusive field of activity, but a qualitatively superior, clearer, more luminous type of consciousness.

The concept of levels of consciousness is not unknown in present-day psychology, but it is not given an adequate meaning and importance because the official mentality of the

Western world remains bound to the idea that only what the senses can perceive, measure, and intellectually classify — the material world, the human body — constitutes reality. The professional psychologist who deals with individuals seeking advice or help has to focus his or her attention upon "the person," which mostly means the field of emotions, interpersonal relationships, and problems arising from an individual's attitude to, and behavior in the family, society, culture, and business world within which he or she is operating. What results from these operations and the emotions they engender is the ego. This ego is the centralizing factor in the consciousness of the person. It is that which is actually implied and even stressed in the little word "I." But this "I" is bound to the physical body, and in most cases to the culture (which means also the religion) and the type of sociopolitical organization in which the person acts, feels, and thinks.

The psychologist deals with this centralizing factor of the person's activities and thoughts-feelings — "I" — mainly at the level of what he or she rather imprecisely calls the psyche; but this psyche is rooted in the functions of the biological organism, the body. All human cultures so far have also been actually based upon biological needs and functions. While religions like Buddhism and Christianity have promoted ideals of asceticism and repudiation of the "desires of the flesh," this downgrading of biological impulses did not greatly alter, at least in Europe, the obvious fact that cultural values remained grounded in biology. What the Christian mentality produced was rather a permanent situation of conflicts, a conflict between human nature (whose drives were considered dark and sinful) and the Soul which God had created once and for all to dwell precariously in the body as a testing ground.

The idea that during one short life-span in a body a Soul could either reach for all time heaven or fall into an ever-enduring hell must be considered the most devilish invention ever conceived to produce psychoneurosis and blighting fear of death. No wonder that, as an inevitable reaction, Western psychology became materialistic and substituted an ego for the Soul! Today the concept of "personhood" embracing body, mind, and spirit in a holistic system, in which every part interacts with every other part, is broadly accepted by the people trying to resolve in their own personal lives the crisis of the society and culture in which they operate. But this solution remains very ambiguous because it does not define adequately or convincingly what mind and spirit basically mean, and the level at which a centralizing factor — vaguely called the self — operates. The "I" is not supposed to be the possessive, aggressive, and separative ego; yet where does it operate from and what is its origin?

Rather than being the *centralizing factor* in the state of personhood in which body, mind, and spirit are theoretically harmonized and interpreted, what is sensed as "I" or called "self" actually is in most cases the product of the ever-renewed conflicts between these three elements of the total personality. Even more than the product of these conflicts, it is *a compensation* (often a rather precarious and at times desperate compensation) for the fact that the consciousness and behavior are the scene of a ceaseless war, at times cold, at others hot and explosive. A person *has to* believe in a Self existing *beyond* the conflicts, even though he or she does not have a clear and workable idea of what is meant by "I" and of the position this "I" occupies in the total person. Such an idea can only take form when we realize that human consciousness should normally evolve from the biological to the sociocultural level, then reach a stage of individualization which, in time and after a long and arduous process of transmutation, should raise the "I" center to a still higher, super-individual level.

We should not speak of self as an individual entity to be taken for granted, but rather *selfhood* as a condition of centralized consciousness and activity which can operate at several levels.

There is a biological type of selfhood rooted in the physical body; it is a power that sustains and operates through all organs and cells of the body. It is the universal life-force operating in a particular manner we call human. It operates in a particular person *through* a genetic code which establishes, first, the basic fact that this person belongs to the human species, then refines its broad generic pattern so that it becomes the genetic code of a particular human being with a relatively unique temperament.

This biological selfhood is very powerful and seeks completely to determine the behavior and the as yet nonindividualized consciousness of the human being. But because it is human the physical organism contains the inherent potentiality of developing a more-than-animal type of group-activity or society — a culture based on a language enabling information resulting from experience to be transmitted to new generations, and leading to the development of a mind able to deal with symbols and general, then abstract, concepts of organization. Selfhood then takes a new form at this level of culture. It becomes what some psychologists now call personhood, but without a clear sense of its relation to biological selfhood and the higher level of individual selfhood.

Any *organized* religion and culture implies some kind of control of biological impulses and desires, and in many instances their complete subjugation in order that the spiritual life-ideal of the religion might be fully developed. Similarly the raising of the centralizing factor in consciousness from the religio-cultural to the strictly individual level requires a process of emerging from *both* the biological and the sociocultural levels. What emerges should be an autonomous, self-motivated, objectively conscious and essentially free (that is, independent) center, not only of consciousness but — as much as it is possible while living in any particular type of society — of activity.

This ideal is now, since Abraham Maslow, associated with the image of a self-actualizing person. But such an ideal is ambiguous. Self-actualized in relation to what? Self-actualization as an end in itself, or as one phase in a process that should extend much further?

The idea implied in most modern psychologies of the person is that personhood is in fact an end-product of evolution. The autonomous, self-actualizing individual actualizes the potential defined by the biology of human nature, and the type of consciousness generated by the sociocultural evolution of mankind as a life-species capable of high mental development. If the concept of spirit is added to that of body and mind, this concept is very unclear. It refers mostly to peak experiences in which feeling of what is called unity with all there is produces an ecstatic consciousness.

Ecstasy, however, literally means "standing outside of oneself." The kind of unity that is felt is far more the unity of an undifferentiated state of being, a return to the prenatal, or even the pre-conception, state — an oceanic kind of unity. Another kind of unity can be reached which does not forget differences, but rather experiences the entire field of differentiated existence and all aspects of consciousness as a synthesized fullness of being. When such a type of experience has become stabilized one can speak of *pleroma consciousness*. In such a state of consciousness all separate "I's" become We — a communion of beings centralized by the totally shared experience of spirit — but not of spirit as an undifferentiated ocean of consciousness: Spirit as it operates at a transindividual level of being.

Pleroma-consciousness and pleroma-selfhood operate at this transindividual level, just as individual selfhood operates at a more than personal, more than cultural and more than biological level. All these modes of selfhood are stages in a process of cosmic and *metacosmic* scope. It is, as the theosophical mind shows us, a broadly cyclic process. Every phase of that process is potential in the fully developed and mature human being. The trouble with modern psychology is that it has become focused on the task of dealing with the distraught members of a Western world in a state of intense crisis — or else, in university laboratories, on the prestigious attempt to cure mental and nervous illnesses according to a sacrosanct scientific method which already postulates the character of the results of the experiments being performed in utterly limiting conditions of investigation, before any results are obtained.

The theosophical world-view should serve as a foundation for a new psychology — perhaps a fifth school of psychology.* It repeats the old Kabbalist statement that man is still in the making. The making of individuals in a conflict-ridden, theoretically democratic and anarchically individualistic society is not the final stage of human evolution. At best it represents only a stage mankind has to pass through on the path to a superindividual and even transphysical level

---

*The so-called "third" and "fourth" schools or forces in psychology, the humanistic and transpersonal approaches, respectively, arose as alternatives to two original directions, Freudian psychoanalysis and behavioristic, experimental psychology.

of being. What is ahead need not be totally unknown, because the process of evolution has a cyclic nature, and each of its phases emerges from the preceding ones in an essentially foreseeable manner.

Unfortunately, the human mind becomes deeply attached to what it has had to concentrate upon during the phase of the process that is reaching its end. The consciousnes to which the collective mind of the culture and religion gave a definite form, and the will whose activities have for a long time operated along a particular track — thus turning into habits — resist change. The creative imagination of most persons is very weak, because the consciousness is filled to the brim with traditional images, names, recipes. Yet time moves on ineluctably, irreversibly. The cyclic process goes on. It cannot be stopped; but individuals, and even an entire civilization, may collapse pastward by refusing in panic to get go of now empty and obsolete beliefs, concepts, and attitudes.

A century ago, H. P. Blavatsky gave us a new vision: a broad, occult vision of cycles and levels of being. The formulation of this vision was conditioned by what the collective mind of Western Civilization could understand at the time. Now the vision should be focused at the level of psychology as well as of social organization. The basic issue is a new approach to the individual — both the individual person and the individual state, nation or culture. The rebirth of humanity is at stake.

Dane Rudhyar is a well-known author to astrological and theosophical readers around the world. His pioneering work in formulating a humanistic — and more recently, a transpersonal — approach to astrology, expressed in over twenty books and more than one thousand articles, has been instrumental in the international resurgence of interest in astrology spanning the last decades. Rudhyar is a respected author of books on philosophy, metaphysics, and the arts, as well as a composer whose works have been performed and recorded. It is through his endeavors in these various creative fields that he has embodied and inspired in many the idea of the Seed Man.

His many books include these Quest books from TPH, Wheaton: *Culture, Crisis and Creativity, Occult Preparations for a New Age, Beyond Individualism: The Psychology of Transformation,* and his latest is *The Astrology of Transformation.*

This article was published in the 1980 Special Spring issue of *The American Theosophist.*

$>$11$<$

THE SOURCE AND THE SEEKER
Jean Raymond, M.D.

> *We shall not cease from exploration*
> *And the end of all our exploring*
> *Will be to arrive where we started*
> *And know the place for the first time.*
>   T. S. Eliot, *Little Gidding*

Man is a social animal. So we are often told. Certainly, as we look at the progress of history, we get the impression that his tendency to socialize becomes stronger with the passing centuries. The population explosion aside, men are deserting the relative isolation of the countryside for a life of crowded confusion in ever-expanding cities. Although this migration may often be prompted by economic reasons, many do not find a better life in the cities, and in fact their lot may be worse. Still they come, often to live in crowded loneliness, squalor, hunger, and violence, somehow nursing a forlorn hope that one day the opportunity will come for them to improve their lot. Money is usually thought of as the key to unlock the door to their dreams — money for better shelter, food, clothing, and luxuries.

For the vast majority of mankind, happiness is equated with such external goals; and this is only natural. Yet, for most, the basic physical necessities are not met, and it has often been said that it is useless to speak to a man of spiritual matters unless his belly is full. But the search for wholeness is a universal one. The fragment is aware of its incompleteness and seeks a remedy in the field of its consciousness and experience. And what is man conscious of, in the main? He is conscious of himself as a separate entity from the world around him, an entity consisting of a physical body, emotions, and thoughts. This is the "I" so far as he knows — all else is 'other.' He is aware of his isolation; he can feel insecure, lost, without a clear idea of how he has arrived at this point, what he is doing here and where he is going. He is not aware, or but vaguely so, of anything else within him that can give him direction and which is stable. All seems to be changing like shifting sand, including that which he considers to be himself — his feelings, thoughts, sensations, even his body. He feels impelled to establish an identity, something relatively permanent to provide him with continuity and security.

Thus arises the great need to 'belong' — whether it is to another person, to a place, a group, or a position. What most people call love is in reality the expression of this need: to possess and be possessed. As a ship at sea throws out an anchor to stop its drift with wind and currents, so man anchors himself to various "not-I's" when he lacks inner direction and purpose. Most people, when asked to identify themselves will do so by listing various relationships — to the place of birth and of residence, to their given name, family, occupation, some accomplishment, and so on — all of which may say very little about the nature of the "self" which has associated itself with all these. Many of these may be changed without altering the self-recognition of the individual involved to any extent. He still retains his awareness that "I am I," that thread of consciousness which gives him continuity. Yet, however obvious this may seem, most men never come to realize it. It seems that the search for wholeness does not have any short cuts for most members of the human race. The process is a long and painful one, in which man is driven by the urge for union, for fulfillment, to take to himself one materialized dream after another, finding each one in turn incapable of giving him the happiness and security he seeks.

It is important to recognize that desire is with us all the way up the ladder. In fact, it is probably necessary as the driving force to make us climb. The "divine discontent" has its source in the sense of incompleteness, the feeling that something is missing. At the more material end of the spectrum, it may manifest in the urge to acquire possessions or power, or in the desire for sexual union. At the spiritual end of the spectrum, there is the desire for freedom from the material world, for liberation, for union with the Divine. The origin of both, however, is the same — the urge of the spark for union with the flame, the dewdrop with the shining sea. The individual may be quite unaware of the source of his urge. He only knows that he is driven by an inner discontent or dis-ease. His attempts to assuage it quite naturally take the forms with which he happens to be most familiar. Thus we find Sri Krishna, representing the Divine Self, saying in the *Bhagavad Gita,* "I am the gambling of the cheat, and the splendour of splendid things am I . . ."[1] The source of man's search for wholeness, no matter where it may lead him, is always the same. It is the "Self seated in the heart of all beings," admittedly obscured and unrecognized by most, but nevertheless the driving force, the very root of consciousness.

We may here enter into a consideration of the constitution of the human being, with its potentialities. There have been many classifications evolved in the religious, philosophical, and scientific fields, certain of them apparently contradictory. Annie Besant's succinct statement on the subject is very helpful: " 'Man' is that being in the universe, in whatever part of the universe he may be, in whom highest Spirit and lowest Matter are joined together by intelligence."[2] Although this classification is probably sufficient for our present purpose, it may be useful to relate it to some of the other ones commonly in use. The correspondence of the familiar spirit, soul, and body triad is fairly obvious, when the word "soul" is used in the context of the "human soul," as HPB called it — the psyche, including both mental and emotional aspects. In psychological terms, there are the super-conscious, the psyche together with its various instinctive and unconscious drives, and the physical body, including the homeostatic and autonomic functions. The Taraka Raja Yoga system, preferred by T. Subba Row, speaks of *Atma* or pure spirit, acting through three vehicles or bases (*upadhis*): 1) *Karanopadhi,* the "spiritual soul," buddhi; 2) *Sukshmopadhi,* the mento-emotional nature or psyche; and 3) *Sthulopadhi,* the dense physical with its etheric ("astral") double and prana or energy field.*

No matter what system of classification one uses for the purposes of study, it must be remembered that man is an integrated being with all aspects interlinked, and it is a mistake to imagine that functionally they can be separated, except in very rare circumstances. Man, strung between two poles of spirit and matter, is the microcosmic reflection of the manifested universe, whose very manifestation is, by definition, dependent upon the interaction between the two poles.

It has often been pointed out that spirit and matter are the positive and negative aspects of the one ever-present reality; that they have no independent existence without each other and apart from the One from which they derive. A graphic analogy often taken is that of the bar magnet with its positive and negative poles. If one cuts off the negative end, the cut surface immediately becomes the negative end, as a result of the fundamental polarity of the bar. No matter where the metal is divided, one is always left with the two poles, positive and negative. It is not just that each cannot exist without the other, but that they are both manifestations of the polarity which is inherent in the whole piece of metal. "There is neither Spirit nor Matter, in reality," says H.P.B., "but only numberless aspects of the One ever-hidden IS (or *Sat*) . . . Matter, after all, is nothing else than the sequence of our own states of consciousness, and Spirit an idea of psychic intuition."[3]

With man, it is neither the "morbid inactivity of pure spirit" nor his material nature that gives him "the capabilities and attributes of Gods . . . for good as much as for evil"[4] (or, we may say, for positive or negative action), but it is the *manas,* the intellect, which makes him self-conscious and capable of

---

*The student will find a useful table giving further correspondences to the five- and seven-fold classifications used in other systems in *The Secret Doctrine* (Adyar six-volume edition, Vol. I, p. 212).

choice. This, the bridge between the two opposites, gives him his unique constitution.

This is probably why the teachings maintain that all entities must pass through the human stage at some point in their evolution. "In order to become a divine, fully conscious god — aye, even the highest — the Spiritual Primeval INTELLIGEN-CES must pass through the human stage, and when we say human, this does not apply merely to our terrestrial humanity, but to the mortals who inhabit any world, i.e., to those In-telligences that have reached the appropriate equilibrium be-tween matter and spirit, as we have now...Each entity must have won for itself the right of becoming divine, through self-experience."[5] And again, Spirit *per se* is an unconscious negative ABSTRACTION. Its purity is inherent, not acquired by merit; hence . . . to become the highest Dhyan Chohan, it is necessary for each Ego to attain to full self-consciousness as a human, i.e., conscious, Being, which is synthesized for us in Man."[6]

We may here recall the tradition that enlightenment can on-ly be attained while in incarnation. The question is often ask-ed why it is not easier to gain enlightenment when free of the dense physical vehicle and in a state of being which appears to be closer to the spiritual source. The foregoing statements may help us to understand this mystery.

The state of enlightenment, cosmic consciousness, Christ consciousness, transformation — call it what we will — is described in remarkably consistent terms by those who have experienced it, when we make allowances for the limitations of language in describing a state which is so beyond the or-dinary consciousness around which language has been built. One of the overwhelming characteristics of this state is the sense of oneness, universality and wholeness. The barriers of the personal self seem to dissolve into the sea of universal consciousness.

"We are to think of the spirit as that part of man's nature in which the sense of unity resides, the part in which primarily he is one with God, and secondarily one with all that lives throughout the universe," says Annie Besant.

> The technical names — by which we, as Theosophists, mark out the spirit — matter not at all. They are drawn from the Sanskirt, which for millennia has been in the

> habit of having definite names for every stage of human consciousness; but this one mark of unity is the one on which we may rest as the sign of the spiritual nature . . . .
> "The man who sees the One Self in everything, and all things in the Self, he seeth, verily he seeth." And all else is blindness. The sense of separation, while necessary for evolution, is fundamentally a mistake.[7]

But we may remind ourselves that the state of enlightenment is a state of *conscious* unity. Spirit without matter is unconscious; to be aware, both are required. The interaction of the two leads finally to their integration and harmonization. H. P. B. points out, "It is only by the attractive force of the contrasts that the two opposites — Spirit and Matter — can be cemented together on Earth, and, smelted in the fire of self-conscious experience and suffering, find themselves wedded in eternity."[8] It appears, therefore, that although the sense of unity derives from the spiritual pole, it must be realized in the body for the transmutation to be complete. To know the One, man must know both spirit and matter, and unite them with the aid of manas.

This brings us to a consideration of how this goal may be attained. We may presume that anything of a separative nature will lead us away from it. Of course, we have been told this repeatedly by spiritual teachers. The question is whether it is generally understood. For example, we find that many injunctions laid down for a so-called spiritual life seem to strengthen the separative and disintegrative tendencies of human nature rather than lead it toward wholeness. The root of the word "whole" is the same as that of "health." Modern psychology is not the first to have recognized that to be healthy, a man has to be integrated, to function as a unit. The separation of body, mind, and spirit as functional entities, which was a fashion for some time, is fortunately now rapidly giving way to the holistic view. It is again being recognized in the healing professions that there is no dis-ease of the body without dis-ease of the psyche, and vice-versa.

Unfortunately, this awareness does not seem to exist in many religious disciplines. Spirituality is often equated with processes of withdrawal, rejection, and repression. The concepts of sin, evil, unworthiness, and pollution are still widespread in religious doctrine and practice, in apparent conflict with the frequent references in scripture to the universality of the God-head, self-existent in every speck of matter throughout the universe. That "in which we live and move and have our being," which is "nearer than breathing, closer than hands or feet," which is the root of all action, and which is "both that which is gross and that which is subtle," is thought to recoil from the material world which is an emanation of Itself.

One may suggest that the concepts of materiality and impurity have become confused. Certainly, for man to develop an awareness of the One, it is necessary for him to detach himself from, or rather to go beyond, the parts, that is, the objects of the senses. But to attempt this by a process of rejection is to defeat the very purpose. The *Light on the Path* states, "If you allow the idea of separateness from any evil thing or person to grow up within you, by so doing you create karma which will bind you to that thing or person till your soul recognizes that it cannot be isolated . . . . And before you can attain knowledge, you must have passed through all places, foul and clean alike . . . the soiled garment you shrink from touching may have been yours yesterday, may be yours tomorrow . . . . The self-righteous man makes for himself a bed of mire. Abstain because it is right to abstain — not that yourself shall be kept clean."[9] Here is pointed out to us the idea that both attraction and repulsion are sources of attachment. Annie Besant remarks, "The true hero of the spiritual life avoids no place and shuns no person."[10]

The point of balance, then, lies in the center. Here, where there is harmony between the opposites, is where there is that which is called non-attachment, which is really a condition of wholeness. Anything which disturbs the balance, whether it be on the one hand the pursuit of objects of desire, or on the other, the attempt to separate oneself from the world, involves expenditure of energy. Attention is required to gain the end sought and to maintain it. Tension is generated, and where there is tension, there is disease, not harmony and wholeness. Whenever the consciousness is involved in a particular activity, whatever it may be, it is not free to move toward universality.

One of the first things a would-be meditator must learn is the ability to relax. He must be able to let go, not only of the tensions of the physical body, but also of the many emotions and thoughts which pull him in different directions. It is fairly easy to understand that relaxation of the physical body involves a letting go of the muscles, and that "trying to relax" leads to increased tension, rather than to relaxation. However, it is not so easy to accept that, in fact, the same law applies to the psychological nature. Trying by a process of effort to quiet the mind and emotions only results in a battle for supremacy which wastes energy and leads to frustration. The ability to let go, to relax, involves a state of acceptance of oneself *as one is,* of complete inner honesty, without the "shoulds" and "oughts" which result in internal dichotomy and external hypocrisy. It is the state of the observer "freed from the pairs of opposites," simply aware in a non-judgmental manner of the processes taking place within the consciousness. "The way is not by dissolving into the limitless space within you."[11] No tension is generated and the consciousness is able to eventually come to rest at the mid-point of the pendulum, the point of balance. Here, where there is no disturbance, it is easy for it to slip into the awareness of its true nature as one with the All.

It is interesting to find that the present-day techniques of Western psychology, called by various names such as centering, self-actualization, individuation, and so on, bear out what the religious teachers have always maintained: that human nature is essentially "good," that is, constructive and integrative. In other words, qualities such as love, kindness, integrity, courage, creativeness, and altruism seem to be "deeper" or more innate, whereas qualities such as malice, fear, greed, and so on are more superficial. The "uncovering" techniques tend to increase the former and to lessen or remove the latter. H.P.B. also remarks that "vice and wickedness are an *abnormal, unnatural* manifestation at this period of our human evolution — at least they ought to be so."[12]

If human nature is naturally good, one look at the world makes us realize that something is very wrong with a society which turns out human beings full of hatred, intolerance, aggression, and selfishness. It is well-recognized that "the child is the father of the man." Man's search for wholeness can be thwarted and distorted for an entire lifetime as a result of his earliest years. With many, sheer physical deprivation may so stunt the growth of body and brain as to make them dull and insensitive. Whether the negative, separative, or the positive, holistic qualities of a character are encouraged in the formative period depends to a very great degree on the adults who surround the individual at that time. Although education has a vital part to play, the pattern may be set long before the child reaches any educational institution, for what happens to him in the first year of life and even in the intra-uterine period, physically, emotionally, and mentally has already conditioned him in his interpersonal relationships and in other aspects of his reactions to his environment. It is obvious, when we look around us, that the vast majority of children will never reach their full potential. One of the most urgent needs today is to try to remedy this situation.

It is encouraging to see that, as a result of the growing realization that the search "without" does not bring fulfillment, there is a growing interest in the search "within." Admittedly, the percentage of the human race touched by this interest is still relatively small. However, each person who succeeds in some measure in finding within himself the point of balance contributes toward a sane society. The integrated individual is also the individual at peace with his environment; he becomes a center for harmony. For the adult, it is often a difficult road, for he has to undo many years of distorted living. But, the child is still close to his center, and therefore everything should be done to make centering techniques available to children. Those who have worked with children along these lines have been able to obtain very positive results. For a sane tomorrow, the children of today must be helped to develop holistically.

We have seen that man occupies a very special place in the universe. By virtue of his constitution, he is the microscopic reflection of the macrocosm; within him lie both heaven and earth; he, and only he, can bring the two together, "smelted in the fire of self-conscious experience and suffering." This is his unique and precious task; the fulfillment of his destiny. The way is through the center — the center which is everywhere.

> *Thus everyman*
> *Wears as his robe the garment of the sky —*
> *So close his union with the cosmic plan,*
> *So perfectly he pierces low and high —*
> *Reaching as far in space as creature can,*
> *And co-extending with immensity.*[13]

References

1. Annie Besant (Tr.), *Bhagavad Gita*, x, 36.
2. Annie Besant, *The Pedigree of Man* (Adyar: T.P.H., 1943), p. 44.
3. H.P. Blavatsky, *The Secret Doctrine* (Adyar: T.P.H.), vol. III, p. 112.
4. Ibid., III, p. 111.
5. Ibid., I, p. 167.
6. Ibid., I, p. 243.
7. Annie Besant, *The Meaning and Method of Spiritual Life* (Adyar: T.P.H., 1916), p. 3.
8. H.P. Blavatsky, Op. cit., III, p. 112.
9. *Light on the Path* (Adyar: T.P.H., 1953), pp. 18, 18.
10. Annie Besant, Op. cit., p. 9.
11. Mary Strong (ed.), *Letters of the Scattered Brotherhood* (New York: Harper and Row, 1948), p. 154.
12. H.P. Boavatsky, Op. cit., III, p. 119.
13. John Charles Earle, "Bodily Extension", *The Oxford Book of Mystical Verse* (London: Oxford University Press, 1917).

Jean Raymond was born in Singapore in 1934. She spent six years of her childhood at the International Headquarters of The Theosophical Society in Adyar, Madras, India. She completed her education in Australia where she earned her medical degree at the University of Sydney in 1958. She was in active medical practice until returning to Adyar in 1971 to assume the position of Recording Secretary (International Secretary) of the Society in which capacity she served until her death in May, 1980. She served the Society in many offices during her long membership and lectured in several countries as well as contributed a number of articles published in theosophical journals. The above article was originally published in the Spring Special Issue of the *American Theosophist,* 1979.

POLARITY AND INTEGRATION

The East discovered the eternal recurrence of the same conditions and similar events. The West discovered the value of the uniqueness of each event or existential condition. The East kept its gaze fixed upon the cosmic background, the West on the individual foreground. The complete picture, however, combines foreground and background, integrating them into a higher unity, the complete human being, the man who has become whole (and therefore "holy"), is he who unites the universal with the individual, the uniqueness of the moment with the eternity of the cyclic recurrence of constellations and existential situations.

In the knowledge of immortality the East neglected the mundane life. In the knowledge of the uniqueness and value of the present moment, the West neglected the immortal. Only in the deepest aspects of the Vajrayana (the Mystic School of Tibetan Buddhism), as well as in the *I-Ching* (the oldest book of Chinese wisdom), the attempt has been made to connect the vision of the foreground with that of the background, to connect the momentary with the eternal and the uniqueness of every situation with ever-recurring constellations of universal forces.

Only he who, while fully recognizing and understanding his Western heritage, penetrates and absorbs the heritage of the East, can gain the highest values of both worlds and do justice to them. East and West are the two halves of our human consciousness, comparable to the two poles of a magnet, which condition and correspond to each other and cannot be separated. Only if man realizes this fact will he become a complete human being. "In man life becomes conscious of itself, and with this it develops into a task and into freedom, so that it can receive anew, make a new start, that it can regain its beginning, its heritage and its origin, and can be reborn." (Leo Baeck)

Lama Anagarika Govinda,
*Creative Meditation and
Multi-Dimensional Consciousness,*
(Wheaton, Il.: Quest), 1976.

More Quest books on transpersonal psychology

And a Time to Die — *Mark Pelgrin*
The author searches for meaning in his own life and approaching death.

The Atman Project — *Ken Wilber*
An added dimensional study of human development.

Beyond Individualism — *Dane Rudhyar*
A journey from ego-hood to self-hood.

The Choicemaker — *E. Howes & S. Moon*
Man's need to make choices as vital to his evolution.

I Wonder Who's in Charge — *Jack Dolan*
Man and his "blaming syndrome" and how to conquer fear and distrust.

The Process of Intuition — *Virginia Burden*
A study of the intuitional principle and how it works.

The Psychic Grid — *Beatrice Bruteau*
How we create the world we know.

The Spectrum of Consciousness — *Ken Wilber*
A view of psychotherapists; the non-duality of spirit; the unique value of all religions.

Storming Eastern Temples — *Lucindi Mooney*
Jungian psychology, Hinduism, and the Amerindian.

Available from:
The Theosophical Publishing House
306 West Geneva Road, Wheaton, Illinois 60187